THE PE

How to Find
The Perfect Boat

and live happily ever after

LIBBY PURVES and PAUL HEINEY

© Libby Purves and Paul Heiney 1987

First published in Great Britain 1987 by
NAUTICAL BOOKS, an imprint of
CONWAY MARITIME PRESS Ltd
24 Bride Lane, Fleet Street
London EC4Y 8DR

ISBN 0 85177 443 1

Cover design by Tony Garrett
Typeset by Inforum Ltd, Portsmouth
Printed and bound in Great Britain by
Oxford University Press Ltd, Oxford

Drawings by Mike Collins

*All characters in this book are fictitious
and none are based on any real persons*

CONTENTS

INTRODUCTION

THERE IS ONLY one secret of happy boating: finding the right boat. However, this takes almost as much concentration as finding the right husband or wife. We speak from experience, being, respectively, a large man of six-foot-two who made the mistake of starting with a very small dinghy, and a chronically unathletic woman who suffered fearful indignities on the trapeze-wire of a Fireball before finding true happiness on big steady keelboats. When you start going on the water, not only must you find a boat at the right price, you must find the right TYPE for you, and identify a member of what you will come to consider the right 'family' of boats.

Like all families, each is made up of individuals with strong points of appearance and character in common. There are the sturdy yeoman family boats and the seductively racy types, the uncomplicated floating planks and the hi-tech wonder machines. Some are fit for loners, and some never seem happy unless crammed with people. Some boats like living in shallow estuaries, and others pine for the deep sea. This diversity is necessary, because sailors (and we include motorboaters) are as diverse a bunch as you could find anywhere. Some are lazy, some are busy, some rich and some broke, some big, small, young, old, timid or brave. For everyone who has a longing to go out onto the water, there is an absolutely right boat somewhere out there; and, sadly, a number of absolutely wrong ones.

Because, alas, enthralling though it is, the great diversity of boats on the market can be a headache. Certainly it leads to a good many wrong decisions, and to the sad sight of numberless craft being bought and then wasted: left unvisited from one year's end to another along the coast.

This small book is an attempt to tell you a few facts about boating which are too basic and universal to appear in most of the other books; and above all to describe the different characters of each family of boats. We take you on a few imaginary voyages to help a first-time buyer to realize what he, or she, actually wants. It would not have been necessary to write it, if every aspiring sailor came from a 'boaty' background or had a wide circle of water-minded friends. The best way, undoubtedly, to

7

find out what you want is to do a lot of trial sailing. This is not always practical; so we have done some of it for you. And although we are only human, and therefore have our own preferences, we have tried fairly to convey the flavour and atmosphere of different types of sailing. We only hope that our frank (and occasionally off-putting) comments will serve their purpose: which is, simply, to warn you off the wrong boat and help you to fall in love with the right one.

We have not listed every boat on the UK market by name – that way madness lies – but we have mentioned some typical, archetypal examples of each family of boats. Armed with these, it is not too difficult to discuss with a reasonable boatyard or dinghy centre exactly what you are looking for, and to understand what the salesman means when he says: 'It's similar to the Wayfarer, only perhaps with a rather easier rig', or 'A lot of Laser sailors graduate to these after a year or so'. In this way, we felt, there would be less risk of our missing out on a new design or ignoring a great change to an old one.

It's almost impossible to indicate prices, so we have not attempted it. But three things are worth remembering. Firstly, that boats depreciate fastest in the first year of their life. A boat one or two years old may be almost perfect but far cheaper than a new one. So remember that if you buy the wrong boat and sell after a short time your loss will be considerable. Secondly, remember that size and price are not always related. Don't get discouraged by the price tag of any single boat at a boat show: it may be of a quality and newness of design which push it way beyond the average. Thirdly, remember the running cost. A good rule of thumb is that you will spend ten per cent of the capital cost of a boat on maintaining and mooring it every year. This figure goes down if you are prepared to do a lot of work yourself from varnishing to engine maintenance; and it goes up if you have a very expensive berth and go crazy in South Coast chandlers. (See Chapter 'Getting the Gear'.)

One other word: some boats on the market genuinely combine several functions and have their roots in more than one boat-family. No sooner had we finished a chapter of this book than we would pass a boatyard, or visit a Boat Show, and spot a genuine hybrid: a fast simple car-top dinghy with room for three people and a picnic, or a camping dayboat with real long-distance potential. Designers are growing very clever indeed at compromise: we take off our hat to them. But, for heaven's sake, be on your guard against any craft advertised as being 'a roomy family cruiser for day or overnight, with a truly Olympic performance under sail, a powerful turn of speed under engine, capable of rugged ocean passages and still easily handled on and off its trailer by a man with one hand tied behind his back'. Nobody should ask the world of one poor boat. But when you do find the right one, the perfect craft for you, you will feel as if you had been *given* the world. On a plate!

WHERE THE WATER IS:

places to sail

NOWHERE IN BRITAIN is more than an hour's drive from some piece of navigable water. Fresh or salt, stagnant or flowing, rocky, muddy, or artificially clear, there is plenty of it. Some of it is free for all, some is tightly controlled by authorities. Some of it the pleasure boats must politely share with commercial shipping and fishing vessels; some is all ours. Here is a very basic breakdown of what's wet:

First there are the inland waterways which divide into canals and rivers.

Canals are man-made legacies from the late eighteenth century before the railways came. The water is kept at a navigable level as they cross the countryside by frequent locks, which you operate yourself (very easy, rather a pleasant job). Most of them are 'narrow canals'; which can only accommodate boats built to the standard traditional narrowboat width (but most locks will take a 76ft long boat, if you have the guts to steer it). There is a speed limit of 7mph or less. Reading between the lines, you will deduce that this is not the place to bring your 30 knot ski-boat, your ton-up wetbike, or your 20ft wide ocean-going motor-sailer. You will also get pretty frustrated trying to tack a sailing dinghy in a narrow canal. However, there are few occupations more beautifully restful than chugging gently through the canal system from North to South, watching new views appearing. One of the nicest things is the way that both town and countryside take on new unsuspected aspects: it is predictably very pleasant to go over a mighty aqueduct across an empty Welsh valley, but more surprising is the pleasure to be gained from creeping round behind the backstreets of Birmingham or Rugby. Most canal boats belong to hire fleets.

Rivers Some sections of some rivers are really very like canals; controlled by locks. But rivers are actually flowing, and may therefore give you a bit more excitement in their lower reaches. There are also hazards such as weirs, and in the weeks after heavy rainfall, great rivers like the Thames can become ungovernably swollen and rapid. Then the water authority will probably ban all navigation for a while.

A greater variety of boats flourishes on the river: sailing, rowing, big and small motorboats exist in reasonably harmony. You need a licence before putting anything onto the water in most places: any dreams you might have had of rafting down the Thames like Huckleberry Finn will probably be cut short at the first lock by a man in a peaked cap with very little sense of humour. The best guide to what you can and can't do on your nearest stretch of water is the Authority responsible; most of these are listed at the end of this book. Also, there will be clubs along the bank that you can observe, or ask. Make sure that if you need to keep your boat in the water, you have a berth arranged and paid for before you are committed; some stretches of waterway are short of berths, and you could end up homeless.

The Norfolk Broads, a system of natural rivers supplemented by old peat diggings, are one of the finest inland cruising grounds in Britain. Plenty of sailing boats, hired and privately owned, use them alongside the motorboats; it is an education in human ingenuity and patience to watch the sailing-boats swing their masts down flat in order to get under the low stone bridges. The most important thing about Broads cruising is to buy, read, and inwardly digest Michael Green's classic *The Art of Coarse Sailing*, and to force yourself to believe that he is not exaggerating, not one bit . . .

At this point we should mention:

Lakes, reservoirs and gravel-pits. More flat, inland water; with the difference that it doesn't lead anywhere. Like a goldfish, you go round and round; this may seem a bit restricting when you are on a four-mile square reservoir (unless you are racing), but if you are gazing at the great sweep of Lake Windermere, you are unlikely to feel cramped. Again, the relevant authority, or the local clubs, are your best guides to individual circumstances.

Getting closer to the coast, we find:

Estuaries. The tidal sections of rivers. The water is still flat, and fairly sheltered, but do not be fooled. Boating can be challenging on estuaries: the tide rips in and out twice a day, mudbanks form sneakily just where you least expect them, and the wind funnels suddenly form

11

unpredictable directions, because it has taken a short-cut between the Power Station and the hill. It is wise to treat a river estuary with the same sort of respect that you treat the open sea. When the wind is against the tide, you even get waves: a special, slapping, choppy kind of water which needs a good sea-boat to cope with it happily. If you buy a very flat-bottomed motorboat, happy on the canals and rivers, you might have an uncomfortable and rather unsafe time on estuary waters. Tell the salesman where you intend to cruise it: no boatyard will knowingly sell you the wrong shape of craft for your real needs.

On the coast, you find different sorts of cruising-ground. There is a broad division between Britain's East Coast, whose characteristics are sandbanks, mud, beguiling little sea-creeks, and few natural harbours but many snug breakwaters built by man; and the West Coast, which is associated more with majestic headlands, huge natural harbours sheltered by mountains, offshore rocks and reefs. But having said that, there are plenty of muddy east-coastlike places in the West (well, look at Morecambe Bay) and some impressive natural harbours in the East (think of Harwich).

Unless you plan to launch a car-topper or a sailboard off the bathing-beach in calm weather (and after checking the speed and direction of the tide, for heaven's sake), you will need a harbour. This may simply mean a concrete slipway 100 yards up a natural creek; or it may mean Plymouth. Harbours, like families of boats, each have a distinct character of their own. Some are combinations of different types, but here are the principal archetypes. You will recognize them without much difficulty.

The Big Commercial Port. There are cranes, and huge jetties under which the tide swirls menacingly; enormous mooring-buoys lie just off the fairway, dwarfed only by the big Trinity house navigational buoys with their diamond topmarks. Barges clank mournfully together, big ships hoot, tugs sheer off at unexpected angles and ferries charge in and out every few hours. If it is a naval harbour, you will row past the sinister dark shapes of submarines and frigates; if it is purely commercial, there will always be a rusting freighter or two bearing a Liberian flag-of-convenience and spewing out brown bilgewater.

None of this means that the BCP is not fit for pleasure boats. It can be enormously exciting, and make you feel part of the wide family of seafarers, to trundle sedately in your 18ft pocket cruiser through the wash of something bound homeward to Valparaiso or Shanghai. It is all a bit nerve-racking for the absolute beginner, but really all you need to know is precisely where you can safely sail, and how to keep clear of the big buoys (steam does NOT give way to sail when that would involve steam demolishing a pier and running aground. Sail gives way to steam, even if that involves a rapid switch-on of the engine and a precipitate flight). It helps to stand for an hour or so in some high position, with a harbour chart, and study the movements of the various ferries and cargo-ships. If you know where they have to go, you'll know not to be in their way. Portsmouth is such a place.

The Naturally Glorious Harbour. Even if it has a big commercial port in one corner, nothing can spoil a natural haven like this. It is vast, set where several rivers meet and protected by high land; you can get in and out at all stages of the tide because there is no sand bar in the way; you have a choice of anchorages, and there is a yacht marina somewhere if you really want a pontoon and company and fuel. There are several yacht clubs, and a good supply of 'visitors' moorings' which may be picked up, and paid for at the clubhouse, by all comers. If it's rough, and you can't face going out for the day, you can sneak up one of the rivers instead. There is really nothing to complain about. Falmouth is one of the best Naturally Glorious Harbours in the country.

The Hard-won Haven. Both of the above have the inestimable advantage of opening directly onto the sea; so that if you want to go anywhere else, it doesn't take much time or planning to get out. The Hard-won Haven is different. Probably because it is a river-mouth, it is obstructed by a 'bar' at the lower states of the tide. If you own a boat with a deep draught (like a fixed-keel sailing yacht or dayboat) you have to think hard about getting in and out; not because the tide in the river is so strong that you can't make any headway against it, but because you need enough water over the bar; you may not be able to get over it except, say, three hours either side of High Water. So your day, or weekend, must be planned with great precision and a tide-table if you are not to find yourself shut out. On the other hand, the harbour is beautifully sheltered in the worst weather and once you are in for the night on a falling tide nobody else can get in and tie up next to you. If you miss the tide out you may well be able to go upriver for some distance instead, or maybe sail around in a broad inland lake which it has formed (like Chichester harbour or, in miniature, Bembridge IOW).

14

The Fishing Harbour. This could be an upriver haven, or right on the coast; the important thing about it is that fishermen are the main, and most privileged users of it. It is not a game to them, boating; it is a living. They may or may not feel friendly towards pleasure-boats in principle; they certainly hate anyone who gets in their way, pinches the berth they need to unload their catch, tangles his propeller up in their nets out at sea, or generally impedes their work. Well, how would you feel about a gang of strangers picnicking in the corridor of your office? Tact and circumspection are necessary in fishing harbours, but many rewarding friendships have sprung up between the professionals and the amateurs in the long run.

The Pretty Yachty Harbour. Here, what fishermen there are have long since resigned themselves to being a quaint tourist attraction. Among all the harbour shops called *Bosun's Locker* and *Mariner's Deli*, among the wine bars and purveyors of garlic paté, there is no-one left who sells anything they need, anyway. There are pretty little stone steps off the pretty little quay, leading to pretty little simple fisherfolk's cottages costing £150,000 and inhabited by commodity brokers; the pub is called the Jolly Something, and you keep expecting the cast of *Howard's Way* to trip round the corner in designer oilskins. We should not sneer, though; it may look like Disneyland to the landlubber, but is still a real harbour, providing real shelter and real places to keep and launch a boat.

SAILBOARDS

standing up to be counted

A LOT OF PEOPLE would argue that this chapter ought not to be here at all, because sailboards are not boats. They have a point: sailboards (often generally referred to as Windsurfers, although this is in fact a trade name) are in a class of their own. The sport does not have much in common with most forms of boating: it is closer to watersports like water-skiing and surfriding. The proof of this is that the boatbuilding industry believes that sailboarders do not, as a rule 'move on' to bigger boats; they move on to better and better sailboards (which means, of course, that you can now buy perfectly good boards second-hand quite cheaply). Also, quite a few board freaks also go sailing or powerboating – witness the number of boards carried on yachts and riverboats, as an extra. One man who does both said that the gulf between sailboarding and boating was roughly the same as the gulf between skateboarding and riding a bike (or motorbike). Sailboards are waterborne skateboards.

However, in their way, they are wonderful; and it could be that you are one of those who prefer them to boats. The important difference between them and skateboards, of course, is that they have not been a short-lived craze: go anywhere in the world and you will see sailboarders skimming or wobbling around on any available water. They do it in the most unpromising conditions; we were very struck by the sight of several chaps on boards in the middle of Muscat harbour, in Oman, where there are hideously poisonous sea-snakes everywhere. One member of the club explained that the seasnakes were a great help to beginners: 'You look down just as you're losing your balance, spot a knot of them writhing around, and somehow you get your balance back ever so quickly'. Something of the same effect has been observed in home waters, when the prospect of plunging yet again into the icy water makes novices really, really concentrate.

And concentrate you must. Sailboarding is all about balance. In a

dinghy, if you misjudge the wind for a moment, your mast is still upright and you are still sitting in the boat. The sails are flapping, but you have another chance. On a board, if you get it wrong you are either heading in entirely the wrong direction (under the pier or up the mud), or else you fall over backwards into the water, and have to grope for the rope attached to your wishbone (the wishbone on your sail, that is, not the one in your neck), and haul the whole soggy shooting-match upright again, with you standing on it. It is very physical. Very hard work. To tack, you have to step round the front of the mast; every manoeuvre the board makes depends on the balance of your body. At the beginning, in an hour's session, you may spend barely ten minutes upright, moving along; the rest of the time puffing and hauling and scrambling and swimming your board around looking for a good place to get back on. As time goes on, you get better; and it is not true that only bronzed slender superheroes and bikini girls can do it. We have seen huge, wobbling middle-aged German bankers managing perfectly well in warm Mediterranean waters; it is a question of application and of enjoying the physical challenge.

Enjoying it depends on several crucial things. Firstly – unless you are exceptional – you will have to learn sailboarding properly. From an instructor. There are countless groups, clubs, and 'schools' for novice windsurfers, and pupils report favourably of them. It is an odd technique to learn, and several things about the physics of it are far from obvious. If the solution to your problem is, for example, to have your hands differently placed on the wishbone, farther back or farther forward, you might as well have an expert to tell you so; otherwise you might spend hours moving your feet, or your weight, or your elbows in and out to no avail, toppling into the water and getting exhausted and depressed.

Secondly, you absolutely must dress right. In home waters, a wetsuit, either with long legs or a 'shortie' version, is essential for 11½ months of the average year. Cold tires you rapidly, and can be dangerous. People do not wear wetsuits in order to look flash (although a lot of men find women in clinging black rubber pretty irresistible); they wear them because water gets trapped between the layers of neoprene, and warms up, forming a snug cocoon around your most vulnerable bits. The cheapest way to get a wetsuit of your own is to buy a kit, with special glue; if you make up your own suit (surprisingly easy and effective) it halves the cost. It only takes an evening.

Thirdly, be safe. Take the water seriously, even if your board is just a new toy. Even if you are warm and confident enough to skip the wetsuit, wear a good buoyancy aid (perhaps even one of lifejacket standard – something which holds your face out of the water even if you are unconscious). And do not go too far from land, especially in an offshore breeze. If something broke, or it got too rough to sail into the wind, you would be nothing but a person clinging to a small plastic plank. The RNLI has an enormous number of call-outs to sailboarders in distress; most of them through sheer silliness.

Used rightly, a sailboard can be wonderful sport, and great therapy. Boards will sail in the lightest of winds, and can cope with quite stiff breezes, so your opportunities for enjoyment are considerable. We know a busy young GP, who sits all day in the surgery or in people's houses, patching up tragedies and placating hypochondriacs, and then goes home to a family of three noisy and demanding young children. He always seems remarkably cheerful on this stressful regime; probably because on the way from surgery to home, he sneaks off to the river with his sailboard and whizzes about for half-an-hour, forgetting the home and the Health Service alike.

CARTOPPERS:

the roofrack pack

QUITE A FEW BOATS will go onto roofracks, if you have enough determination (the authors have experience of pushing a 16ft clinker-built rowing-boat on to the roofrack of a Ford Transit, but would not attempt it again); but what we are talking about here are the lightweight, flattish, plastic dishes that one person can handle without grunt or strain. They are a breed apart from other boats: the first time you see a one-man car-top dinghy you might be forgiven for thinking that it had been invented by an exhausted sailboard addict, who decided that he wanted to sit down. Indeed, these boats are almost as basic as the simplest sailboard (although naturally, their masts are rigid rather than hinged, since there is no-one standing up there to hold them upright). But in fact, they predate the sailboarding craze: light, buoyant, immensely strong plastics gave birth some years ago to the concept of the plastic car-top dinghy.

They are not boats that Arthur Ransome's Swallows and Amazons would recognize. The simplest cartoppers have only one sail, and no stays to hold the mast up. You do not sit in them, you sit *on* them, using various cunningly placed loops and straps to stick your feet in. They move off across the water with great dispatch in the lightest of winds, are responsive to the slightest twitch of your wrist on the helm, and capsize if you aren't careful. In fact, even if you are careful, a freaky puff of wind might have you in the water any time; a wetsuit and a buoyancy aid are definitely desirable in our bracing climate. Nor is it advisable to venture too far offshore without a rescue boat close at hand; or to get yourself into the sort of situation where you might have to row home. Few cartoppers have room for more than a plastic paddle.

Allowing for these obvious limitations, a cartop dinghy can be magic. You get to the waterside, undo a couple of straps, fit the mast (and sometimes the sail, all in one movement), adjust a couple of lines,

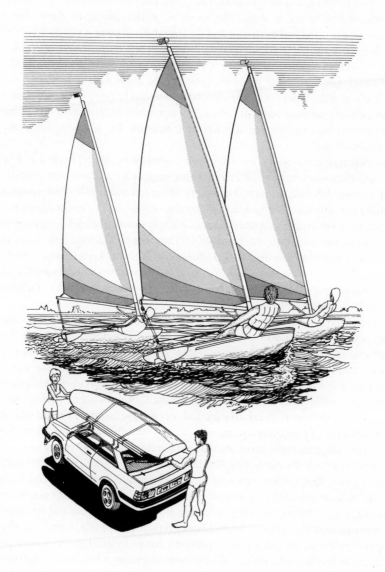

wriggle into the appropriate clothing and presto! you are on the water, within five minutes. And off you skim, with nothing to think about except the wind and the water and the tiny shifts of your weight and of the sheet in your hand which make all the difference to the flying plank's performance. You can feel the water thrumming, not only through the rudder and tiller, but through your whole body as it balances in the shallow dish. There is a centreboard which can be adjusted up or down depending on your point of sailing, but not much else to fiddle with. This is pure sailing; on the face of it, a simple business, but allowing for many levels of skill.

Naturally, these boats are raced enthusiastically. There are few modifications you can make to anything so simple – although some of the Laser models have grown alarmingly advanced and subtle, with control lines for adjusting the sail shape – so class racing can be enthralling; the man who overtakes another in an absolutely identical dinghy, out of the same mould and with spars and sail off the same production line, really is entitled to claim he is the more skilful sailor. Another keen group of users are older children and young teenagers, who revel in the speed and freedom and solitude, and in being able to launch and recover the boat easily without help.

However, a new group of car-topper sailors is emerging: not racing types, nor particularly young. One property developer, a man in the stressful and successful 'fifties, told us how he takes his Topper everywhere on the roofrack of the company car, and flings it in the water on his way home from site meetings by the coast; he pays a subscription to three different reservoirs in the Home Counties so he always has somewhere to stop and skitter around, even in the lashing rain and hail of midwinter. Then there are parents with young babies, who go to the water's edge and take turns at sailing around while the other one sits and watches beside the pushchair; half the beauty of energetic, wet little boats like this is that twenty minutes thrashing around in a good wind feels almost as much of an adventure as sailing a big comfy cruiser across to France. It's a bit like playing squash: concentrated exercise and stimulation in a very short time. When Daddy returns, dripping slightly, to the pram or the car's front seat, he is perfectly happy to let Mummy have a go while he listens to the radio and plays with the baby. One couple said that a Saturday routine of an hour on the water between them, a bag of Eccles cakes and a thermos of tea did more to uphold their marriage in the first two years of parenthood than anything else.

Of course, some car-toppers carry two people; at least one on the market, the Laser Fun, can accommodate two adults and a child of seven or so, and has a foresail, in a remarkably light and compact craft. It has to be said, however, that it still capsizes almost as easily as the others, and anyone strapping a picnic-hamper to it and heading for distant shores is risking his sandwiches. More awful risks are run by anyone who thinks he – or she – needn't bother with the wetsuit and the lifejacket. Think of it as a comfortable sit-down Windsurfer, and you won't go far wrong. Fun is the word.

FAST DINGHIES:

all zing and string

AH, NOW THIS ONE looks more like a boat. We are still not quite in Wind-in-the-Willows country, though; Ratty and Mole never took a picnic out in anything quite like this.

Imagine a trip: Climbing aboard, cautiously (there is almost nowhere to sit, and she tips easily), the first thing you notice is string. A spaghetti-like profusion of the stuff, in various colours and textures, leads all over the cockpit through various fairleads and jamming-cleats which look like tiny black plastic dentures. Some of them are merely the usual sheets and halyards, but most of them are specialized tensioners and adjusters for changing the shape of the sail, flattening it here and slanting it there; for adjusting the rigging-tension or raking the mast for optimum performance. Some of the strings belong to the spinnaker, which is lurking down a plastic chute at the bow, waiting to be whisked up in seconds; some of it belongs to the trapeze, of which more later.

The owner of this intimidating machine is sitting in the stern, fussing about the shape of his centreplate. Let us call him Kev Lahr. Let us assume the boat to be that racing classic, a Fireball. Kev has been having an argument with someone else in the class (these boats are seldom found singly; they thrive in large and aggressive racing classes, like Finns and Flying Dutchmen), and his hated rival has told him that he reckons shaving a millimetre off the bottom of his centreplate has reduced 'tip-drag' and added approximately 0.05 of a knot to his average speed through water. This has sent the owner into a frenzy of indecision: is it true? is it a clever bluff by his rival? is it, in fact, legal within the racing rules? He is in two minds about whether he can, after all, spare the time to give you a sail before the race begins. He does not, of course, want you aboard during the race itself, because he has a regular crew: a tough, slight boy of fifteen who is as dedicated to winning races as he is.

However, he finally casts off his mooring-lines and sets about

24

instructing you in your duties as his crew. Slowly, you work out which piece of string is which, and refrain from asking him why all his tensioners and their cleats are so cunningly placed to stop you getting comfortable. There is a very good reason for this: the boat's speed is about fifty times more important than your comfort, or even his. Everything in this boat is geared for speed; looking over the side, you find to your slight surprise that she is already travelling at a considerable pace, although the wind is barely perceptible. You follow Kev's slightly impatient instructions for setting the spinnaker – which goes up easily enough – but take some time to manage the tricky business of gybing the pole from one side to the other when the helmsman changes direction to put the wind on the other quarter. This is not helped by the fact that you have to move right forward on this light and unstable platform, and stand up to do it. Once the sail is set, however, you realize why the hull is the unstable shape it is: in order to plane. A puff of wind in the spinnaker, and suddenly the whole feeling of the boat changes; it lifts, and seems to fly across the surface of the water rather than ploughing through it. You are now going very fast indeed, in hardly any wind, and everything is happening very rapidly. The owner has a look of rapt, happy concentration on his face, broken only by the odd grimace when he remembers his tip-drag dilemma. He is also worried by the way in which you are sitting so happily looking around you and enjoying the view. You ought to be tweaking at the sails, or watching for puffs of wind on the water, or eyeing up the rest of the fleet, or getting the trapeze-gear ready.

Back on the wind again, the boat is now heeling far too much for comfort or efficiency. Well, never mind comfort. Efficiency is more important: her fastest sailing will be done with the Minimum Wetted Area, which means she must be kept nearly upright. You are both already sitting out, him with the tiller-extension gripped in his hand. He is very proud of this tiller extension; he made it himself out of some material so new and so lightweight as to be nameless, and hollowed it out further in order to save weight. It breaks once a week.

In order to get upright, you now have to get out onto the trapeze. The owner would volunteer to do this himself, only he knows perfectly well that if he gave you the helm of this spirited little surf-board, you would make a mistake or two, which would result in him getting a very cold and sudden bath. So he stays put, and instructs you in how to become a marine trapeze-artist instead. You are already wearing a sort of canvas nappy over your clothes, with a big eye just at waist level; there is a wire coming down from the top of the mast with a corresponding clip on it. All you have to do is clip on, step boldly out into the flimsy side-deck of the boat (if you are lucky, he has put some form of foot-gripping rubber mat on it) and throw yourself backwards, relying on the wire to hold you in place. Your correct position, since the wind has freshened, is lying backwards parallel to the speeding water, and about a foot above it. On no account allow your forward leg to bend at the knee, or you might dangle suddenly forwards and wrap yourself around the forestay. Nor should you neglect to watch the helmsman and the wind in the sails closely; he may forget, in all the excitement, to tell you when your function as outboard ballast is about to become redundant. Also, do not forget, when tacking, to alter not only the jib-sheet from port to starboard, but the trapeze wire as well. There is nothing more embarrassing than finding yourself clipped to the wrong side when it is too late to change, and the sails swing across leaving you shackled to the leeward side. You will capsize the boat.

After a few tacks, you may be enjoying the sensation of flying over the water, swinging out on the trapeze, balancing the boat and managing the string and the spinnaker, all at once. But it is worth asking yourself whether your proposed crew – wife, child, husband, whoever – is going to feel the same way when you actually buy one of these nervy, racy boats and expect a similar crew service. You can't race one without a crew, they're not made for having picnics aboard, and a capsize is not only possible but extremely likely. Musing on all this, you forget to change your trapeze-wire across on a tack, and manage to turn the boat over. The owner is not pleased, and appears from the other side of the wallowing hull to glare at you. He rights the boat with considerable ease – it's built for such incidents – and shoots off downwind with his transom-flaps draining the water out at incredible speed. You are expected to carry on tweaking the sails as if nothing had happened. The owner begins to talk about the latest Olympic trials of his class or the nearest similar one to qualify.

At this stage, two things may happen. You may painlessly decide that this boat is not for you: too highly-strung in every sense, too demanding of concentration, too precarious for much family fun, and too dependent on a keen crew. You may decide to investigate the less 'hot' classes, which are happy to cruise as well as race. Or you may fall in love with the boat, beg for a go on the helm, and become fascinated by the infinite subtlety, the speed and the grace and the science of it all. You may resolve to own such a boat, and swear to race her on every possible weekend so as to pit your personal science and skill against others. You may warm to the owner, and long humbly to be able to argue the finer points with him in the club hut over a beer. If so, you are a fast-dinghy person, and need look no further. Unless you decide to go farther still down the road of speed, and examine the abilities – breathtaking abilities – of the ultralight racing catamaran-dinghies with two hulls instead of one.

Only one word of warning. You may have fallen in love with the right type of boat, but the wrong class. Your local reservoir, or coastal sailing club, may be committed to quite another model. In this case, there is little point in buying an alien dinghy unless you are prepared to trail it across country to the nearest competitive fleet. Handicap racing (between different classes) does happen; but there is a particular edge to racing against an identical boat which nothing else can match.

Incidentally, it could be that you fall in love with the racing ideal, and the subtleties of a finely-tuned and infinitely tweakable sailing rig, but are reluctant to face the repeated duckings and capsizes involved in learning to manage a fast centreplate dinghy. It may be that you are the perfect crew or helmsman for one of the great racing keelboat classes: the Dragons, the Darings, or the Flying Fifteens. These do not capsize, having heavy fixed keels; but they are very fast indeed and sailed with great dedication and concentration, right up to Olympic level in some cases. Pricey, but many are owned by syndicates, and quite a few by rich owners who are always hopefully on the lookout for good crews – who will probably have graduated from racing dinghies.

STEADY DINGHIES:

family friends

ONE OF THE TRICKIEST distinctions to make is between racing boats and small cruising dinghies. For one thing, some of the steadiest, friendliest little pottering boats manage, in the hands of keen owners, to form highly competitive racing classes; for another thing, it is often true that yesterday's hot racing dinghy is today's family boat. One of the nicest picnics I ever went on involved three adults and two toddlers in an ancient Enterprise; in her time, she had been champion of all Ireland, but, sailed circumspectly, was equally fit for our modest expedition.

However, if you want a rule-of-thumb, I consider a Family Friend to be a dinghy which carries oars aboard, and is humble and good-natured enough to accept an outboard motor being fixed on her stern occasionally. She should also have cubby-holes enough to stow a dry sweater or two for the kids, and several hooky fishing-lines for mackerel. One of the smallest is the famous Mirror dinghy, designed by Jack Holt and Barry Bucknell over 25 years ago as a D-I-Y boat for all purposes. The revolutionary stitch-up construction, the stubby flat bow and gracefully bowed bottom, made her distinctive; the gunter rig kept the spars short and manageable. Two adults and a child can sail in a Mirror, provided the adult sitting under the boom does not mind a bit of hunching-up; under outboard, with the mast out, another adult could join them in calm waters. It is not surprising that the boat survived so long, and is now reproduced in glassfibre (although the reason for the odd shape, the construction method, is no longer relevant in GRP). Mirror No. 1 is now flaunting her red sail in the National Maritime Museum at Greenwich; her enduring success is the same sort of tortoise-and-hare story as the longevity of the Citroen 2 CV 'tin snail' car.

However, most of the steady, family dinghies are a bit bigger than the Mirror's 12ft. You can get a Mirror on top of a car, at a pinch; most of the bigger ones (up to 15ft) need trailers. And the bigger they get, the more

they overlap into the next family of boats, the hardy camping dayboats.

But a Family Friend is, essentially, modest in its ambitions. You are not really likely to use it as an overnight camping boat – although Margaret Dye does, notably, go off for days in her Wanderer with a tent on top. You are not likely to set out round Britain in it (although, Heaven knows, even as we write someone is probably attempting it). You just want a nice, safe, sail and a trouble-free trail home.

So what is it like to sail in? Suppose you are invited out in their 15-foot dinghy by the Rollock family: Ken and Betty, plus young Tom who is seven. The boat, in this case, is wooden – prettily built in clinker style, with overlapping planks. They find it a bit heavy to get on and off the trailer, and it is beginning to leak a bit; also the annual revarnishing takes up much of Ken's winter leisure, and all of his carport. Still, they have had the *Rollocker* for six years now, ever since Tom was one, and despite the lure of maintenance-free lightweight GRP, they can't quite bear to part with her.

They launch off a club slipway into a wide East Coast river. Since the wind is favourable and light, they hoist both sails on the slip, and let them flap idly while they load up a waterpoof sailbag containing the picnic and a few spare woollies. Being a guest, you are bundled aboard with dry feet, together with Tom, while his parents wade into the water in wetsuit-socks to push the boat off. They used to wear high yachting boots, but found that one false step off the bottom of the slipway into the mud, and their feet would stay soggy all day. Both of them climb aboard and you glide off easily with the wind on the beam, sliding sideways rather a lot until Betty gets the centreplate down. A few minutes are spent in such adjustments as hauling down the boom with the kicking-strap, moving the port jib-sheet which young Tom has accidentally led through the wrong gap in the rigging, and finding a piece of spare lashing in the glory-hole under the helmsman's seat to reinforce the doubtful fixing on the tack of the mainsail. All this is done at leisure, and in good humour; nobody is hoping for record speeds today, especially not with Tom in proud sole charge of the jib.

You have a flood tide under you, so head upriver for a pleasant gravelly beach near a church Betty has always meant to visit. The tide will turn at lunchtime, and bring you gently back. The Rollock family used to sail this boat on a reservoir in Oxfordshire, before they moved, and have trailed it up to the Lakes; but they find the tidal river most invigorating. As Ken says, with a strong ebb tide and the wind against you in the good old *Rollocker*, you can beat hard for half-an-hour upstream and at the end of it not even have the bother of sailing home, since you will still be only ten feet upstream of the slipway. If they intend to go anywhere, they go with the tides.

Betty tacks hurriedly to avoid a wobbling Windsurfer, and little Tom forgets to uncleat the jib from the new windward side and make it up to leeward; the jib lies aback for a moment, until Ken frees it, but despite a freshening wind the little boat with her straight keel is very forgiving, and settles down rapidly after the kerfuffle. Later on, a sudden gust hits her as she is creaming along close-hauled; it might have tipped an unwary car-topper right over, but even though Ken is actually trying to get an arm into his jersey at the time, and steering with his knee, all that happens is that a cupful of water comes aboard over the lee rail and Tom decides it is time he 'sat out' to windward.

You take the helm. The boat is responsive, but not as light to steer as the racy dinghy or the car-topper; if you let the tiller go, she rounds up good-manneredly into the wind, awaiting further instructions. If you fell overboard, the boat would probably not go very far away from you. On the other hand, she is not big, and does not have draining-flaps at the back like a racer; climbing back in could be a wet, tippy business and mean a lot of work with the baler. If she were to be swamped, she would float: any boat worth her salt has 'positive buoyancy', either built-in by means of air trapped in hollow moulded or wooden sections at the bow and stern, or else – as in the case of this old boat – provided by discreet white PVC buoyancy-tubes fixed under the seats.

Crunch. Up on the gravel beach she goes, down come the sails, and her crew climb out for the picnic and the walk (remembering to pull her up above the high water mark). An hour later, the ebb tide has set in nicely, and with fair wind the Rollocks decide not to bother hoisting the mainsail at all. Under jib alone they head downstream, with Ken and Tom hopefully trailing fishing-lines over the side. The wind drops, and drops further; Betty is getting cold, so puts the mainsail back up for a little more speed. A sail-batten falls out, but nobody can be bothered to put it back just now, so a slightly fluttering-edged mainsail pulls the boat home. Not quite the stuff for the Royal Ocean Racing Club newsletter, but who cares, as long as you're happy?

It is colder; feet are wet; the rain begins to fall, and waterproofs are pulled out of their hiding-places in the bow and donned. Nobody is sorry when the slipway comes in sight around the last bend; a cup of hot coffee and a bun ashore is a very welcome prospect. Up goes the boat, with a certain amount of effort, onto her trailer, and the family head homeward.

Of course, nothing stands still in family life. These have been six happy years, but if the Rollocks buy a new boat, they are seriously considering some changes. Tom wants his own boat, and they are thinking of an Optimist (a baby version of the Family Friend type, and one of the finest solo teaching boats for children afloat). Ken has inherited a couple of thousand pounds, and is wondering whether it would be a good idea to get a slightly bigger boat, with a cuddy, so that the hot cup of coffee could be achieved without getting ashore. They might even try sleeping aboard, while Tom is on his Optimist training weeks with the Island Cruising Club. Meanwhile, the *Rollocker* bounces serenely along behind the car; a good friend, always there when they want her, and not too much bother when they don't.

The choice of Family Friend dinghies is enormous. There are outdated racing boats often going cheap; purpose-built family cruising dinghies by the dozen; and – one of the most pleasant developments of the past decade – an ever-widening range of reproductions of traditional boats in this size. A Cornish Shrimper or Coble, or one of the smaller Drascombe boats, combines the security and prettiness of a traditional fishing-boat with the ease of GRP and Terylene and nylon ropes. And there are enough of them around to rally and race, if you fancy the occasional burst of competitive activity.

Finally, if you are nervous of trailers and roofracks, and can't leave a boat permanently on a mooring or mudberth all summer, it is worth remembering a relative newcomer to this family of boats: the sailing inflatable. This is no relation of the superfast miniature catamarans with inflatable hulls which are part of the zing-and-string category of boats; it is a well-behaved dinghy about 12ft long, capable of holding two adults and a child, and of being rolled up in a car boot at the end of the day. We own one, a Tinker Traveller, and although it is a fairly expensive way of buying a 12ft boat, have had great fun out of it in our very limited free time. The bigger, better-stiffened models sail perfectly well, even hard to windward; but the great thing is to remember to pump them up really, really hard; otherwise the rigging goes slack, and their sailing qualities approximate closely to those of a square-rigged banana skin.

CRUISERS WITHOUT DECKS:

the hardy dayboats

WHEN FRANK DYE sailed his 15ft Wayfarer dinghy to Iceland and wrote a stirring book about it, he was perfectly illustrating the way that the divisions between boat 'families' can get blurred. Before Dye, we would have placed Wayfarers unhesitatingly at the head of the previous dynasty: big, steady, faithful family friends which would take you out sailing by day and stay securely on their moorings or trailers at night. What Frank Dye proved is that with a bit of determination, a well-designed 15ft open boat is perfectly capable of night passages and open sea crossings – as long as it is sailed by a consummate and experienced seaman. Most of the cruising dayboats we are talking about are actually a few feet bigger than the Wayfarer – but all the same, few of us would sail them to Iceland. It is a question of seamanship and daring.

The other thing to notice is that quite a few of the bigger sailing dayboats (that is, boats without a cabin, or with just a little cuddy to shelter from the rain), are actually longer and almost as expensive as the smallest 'pocket cruisers', which *do* have habitable cabins. Why, then, does anyone want an open boat 20ft long when they could have a miniature yacht? Several reasons. One contented owner of a Drascombe Lugger explained succinctly: 'Want to fill the boat with fish, mucky old nets, friends with long legs. Lot of room in an open boat, not much room if you put some titchy cabin on. Also, let's face up to it, fish and friends both make a boat filthy. I like to be able to turn a hose on it, sluice it out'. If he goes off for several days, he just puts the camping tent up at night, and by day keeps his oilskins handy.

There is something very appealing about a big, solid, open boat. These are designed never to capsize unless in extreme (and avoidable) conditions; they are proper sea-boats, fit for coastal voyages several miles from land, and you can stand up and move around in them without wobbling. It is possible for them to have a large, permanently fitted outboard (or

even an inboard) engine, without affecting their ability to sail. Some of them have made great voyages all over the world – coasting voyages, with frequent port stops, but nonetheless adventurous. Webb Childs took a Drascombe Lugger round Cape Horn; Dye's Wayfarer voyages earned his boat *Wanderer* a place in the National Maritime Museum. On a less ambitious level, these big hardy dayboats are the sort to coax family members afloat who would be nervous in a smaller craft, and who dislike the extreme heeling-over of a performance boat sailing to windward. Passengers relax, and enjoy the scenery, instead of bracing themselves nervously for the next lurch.

Suppose we take a sail, with Dan Transom and his girlfriend Helen. They have a 19ft open boat (named *Emma* after a previous girlfriend, although Helen always pretends it was named for Nelson's lady friend). *Emma* is made of glassfibre and fitted with a 25 horsepower outboard on a lifting bracket which holds it clear of the water when sailing. She is a yawl, a two-masted craft with a small sail on a low mast behind the helmsman's seat. Dan pulls the boat behind his medium-powered saloon car on a trailer; when we meet him, he is beside a harbour slipway in Weymouth, starting a week's holiday. His bible is a book called *Where to Launch Your Boat*, as he has discovered the hard way that unlike his old 13ft dinghy, which could be slithered over the mud at a pinch, this boat needs a hard concrete slip to be launched and recovered.

It takes him and Helen twenty-five minutes to get the waterproof covers off and the masts rigged. Because they invested in a good cover, all that they need for a couple of days afloat is left permanently stowed in the many lockers around the boat; lifejackets, signal flares for emergencies, waterproofs, a stock of tinned food, plates and cutlery, and a small primus stove. They have become extremely good at devising water-proof stowage schemes – even the tea-bags survive, in a plastic box inside another plastic box containing a dessicant sachet – but even so they are prudent enough not to leave their sleeping-bags aboard when they aren't living on the boat.

Half-an-hour after stopping, then, Dan backs the car cautiously down the slip until the trailer is partly underwater; then unhooks it and slides the boat and trailer further down, to haul the trailer out from under when the boat begins to float. His least favourite slipways are the ones which treacherously stop, just below the low-water mark; there are few things worse than a trailer stuck firmly in the mud with the weight of a boat still partly resting on it. He detaches the bow of the boat from its winch-wire and parks the trailer out of the way while Helen holds the bow-line; then Dan hops in, throws a rope to Helen on the little pier close by, and they politely bring the big boat alongside for you to step aboard in comfort.

The idea is to sail to Lulworth Cove for the night, some eight miles east of the harbour mouth. As the wind is fluky, Dan decides to motor out of the river, and set sail once he is clear of the anglers trailing their lines from the big pier's end, the incoming Channel ferries, and other hazards. Once outside the harbour mouth, the wind seems to fill in from the South-east, giving him a fairly narrow reach to Lulworth, with the sails hauled quite close. The swell is noticeable, and the waves slapping the starboard bow might have stopped a smaller boat or made her pretty uncomfortable; but *Emma* has little trouble with a sea this size, and ploughs on at a good five knots, with her heavy centreplate fully down to prevent her making any leeway towards the rocky coast. With Portland Bill looming astern, and the coast over a mile away to port, this feels like a real sea voyage; they have taken the boat on the Lakes, on the Broads, up countless rivers, but always get an extra edge of excitement from a sea crossing. Last year, Dan recalls, they sailed from Cornwall to the Scillies for their holiday, and spent an idyllic week diving and fishing and exploring, sleeping the night either in the boat or in their pup tent alongside her on the beach. The weather deteriorated sharply on their last Saturday, however, a gale blew up, and Dan decided to arrange for the boat to be hauled up onto the *Scillonian* ferry to get back to the mainland, and within reach of his car. 'Now you couldn't have done that with a stormbound yacht, could you?' he brags, showing round a photograph of the blue boat sitting smugly on the ferry's deck.

Counting hills, examining cracks in the rock, Helen identifies the entrance to Lulworth Cove, and the sheets are freed off for the boat to run in towards the coast. With the sea behind her, the crew are grateful for her buoyant stern which lifts easily over the waves, and lets none of them aboard. She really is an excellent seaboat. In the coasts, between the cliffs, she crosses the horseshoe cove. With the centreplate pulled up, and the mainsail dropped, the helmsman is able to guide her gently up onto the sandy beach. A quick haul, and she is steady above the tideline.

A night aboard is in prospect: there is some discussion as to how to arrange matters. Dan is in favour of anchoring the boat out in the cove, with the bigger yachts, and sleeping there at anchor. Helen likes the solidity of the beach. Eventually, it is decided to sleep out at anchor, since the wind has dropped; the boat is rowed out, the anchor dropped and bedded well in, and they begin the job of putting up the camping-tent – a sort of green tunnel with sealable pointed ends. It takes about a quarter of an hour, and once it is up the boat is transformed. Waterproof cushions appear out of glory-holes, the little stove is set up in its holder, and a pleasant fug develops as the evening cools outside. With a bit of scuffling and rearranging, the little canvas cabin is turned into a kitchen lit by a gently glowing gas-lamp, then later into a snug bedroom. Dan and Helen have to lie either side of the centreboard-case, with 50lb of steel plate between them; Helen's mother considers this entirely appropriate to their unmarried status.

On the whole, when it comes to sleeping out, the couple consider their boat more convenient and comfortable than a tent but less so than a cabin cruiser. They don't want to get involved in all the expense and complication and maintenance of a miniature yacht with plumbing and heating and navigational systems – Dan considers his working life quite complicated enough without embarking on complicated leisure – but they have thought about getting a similar boat to their own, from the same manufacturer, which has been equipped with a cuddy. This is a tiny covered cabin in the bow, holding two bare bunks and a shelf for cooking on; it would mean that they could sit below in turn and make cups of tea under way. This would also be of some assistance to Helen in the delicate matter of relieving herself; the farther offshore and the more adventurous the voyage, the more pressing the problem has become. Seventy years of female emancipation are no help at all in this extremity; men can still stand carefree by the leeward shrouds, gazing at the horizon, while for a woman to pee off an open boat requires ingenuity, determination, and a sense of humour. Given a discreet cuddy to go into, a perfectly adequate and modest bucket-and-chuck-it system is made possible – if not the wild, unthinkable, luxury of a miniature chemical toilet.

These reservations apart, you can have a happy spartan holiday aboard a Lugger or a Dabber or an Explorer or a Wayfarer. They are easily beachable, and have a very shallow draught with the centreplate up; so you can explore the tiniest creeks and inlets. Also, you can always find a snug place to hide up on the shore on windy nights, while the yachts which depend on mooring or anchoring are yawing around wildly in the bay. The permanently rigged motor is a blessing if you get caught out in a calm, yet still unhooks and can be carried up to a garage if it goes wrong; the sailing is safe and exhilarating, and there is enough space for children, dogs, and other non-participant members of the crew not to be constantly underfoot. As Dan and Helen winch the boat back onto her trailer with practised ease (it took them half-a-dozen launches and recoveries before they did it without shouting at each other, but now all is serene), they suddenly get the idea of trailing the boat over to Ireland on the car ferry, and exploring the islands of the far west; the topic keeps them happy for the whole drive home.

POCKET CRUISERS, BABY RACERS, TRAILER-SAILERS:

keeping your head down

WHEN CHOOSING WHAT has become known as a 'pocket cruiser', look over your shoulder and repeat to yourself *Caveat Emptor*: Buyer Beware! There is something about small cruising yachts, that is those between 17 and 25 feet, that makes boat salesmen depart from their usual straight and narrow wake. This is an area where you really must know what you intend to do with your new boat; otherwise you are in for either an uncomfortable or an unnecessarily expensive time.

Take as an example the new, imaginary, Eddystone 21. In the advertising brochure we see her broad-reaching on a sunny day in a Force 3, big smiles on the face of mum and the kids, dad wearing his 'rugged helmsman' stare. We read how she's an ocean-crossing yacht, but also an ideal day-sailer, club one-design and perfect on a trailer. She'll even sleep six.

You'll be lucky indeed if she does more than two out of the five things claimed for her. Not that they are deliberately trying to mislead you; she may well cross oceans, if you happen to be called Slocum. It's a bad boat indeed that you can't bear to sail for a whole day so the 'ideal day-sailer' claim can be ignored. She may well be a club one-design if you happen to moor her near to the right club. Trail and sail her by all means, providing you have a car with a five-litre engine to get her deadweight up the hills. And she may well sleep six, providing they are stacked in a neat pile! Pocket cruisers are so called because you live in one another's pockets. The point is this: ask yourself which of those characteristics is most important to you and look for a boat that measures up to that. If she turns out to have any of the other qualities as well, think yourself lucky.

Let's look at 'ocean' potential first of all: it's the notion of being safe and comfortable at sea that has caught your eye. You may not have a Pacific or Atlantic crossing in mind, your ambition might be a Thames Estuary cruise or a Mounts Bay crossing, but you want to feel that, skilfully handled, your boat is going to get you places. A good technique is to look first of all at big yachts, 35-footers and above, even though you can't afford them: and *then* at the little one you fancy, and see if you spot any similarities. Does she have some strength to her or has she got the 'masted caravan' look? If she has, she probably sails like a caravan and probably will sleep six at the expense of more windage than is safe on the open sea. It is true of all boats that if they look right, they are right; and so if you see a hint of scaled-down ocean-yacht about her, you are heading in the right direction.

Look at the weight of the fittings and how they are fastened to the boat. You certainly won't need winches as heavy as the ones on the big boat; they have large sail areas to handle. But the lifelines need to take as much strain on a 20-footer as on a 40-footer (a few boatbuilders seem to consider the lives of small-boat owners more dispensable, and use lighter fittings than on bigger craft). And if you spot that the stanchions have only been secured with easy-to-rip-out, self-tapping screws, ask yourself how well put together the rest of the boat might be. Imagine her at sea in a fresh breeze and leaning over twenty degrees. How comfortable will she be then? The bowl of fruit that makes its annual appearance on the saloon table at the Boat Show (presumably placed there to persuade the hesitant buyer that sailing is just like sitting at home, but on water) may well have slid into the side bunks by now and reduced itself into a purée to await the first person to come off watch. Will you still be able to boil a kettle for tea and steady yourself sufficiently to slice a wedge of nourishing fruit cake to feed to the flagging helmsman? If such concerns smack of molly-coddling, and you believe them to have no place in the gritty business of bouncing and crashing from one wave to the next with the utmost haste, you are not a cruising type and you should look for a boat which has the word 'racing' somewhere in its description, and stick to thrashing round the buoys on a Saturday afternoon. Out at sea, on passage, comfort should not be thought of as an indulgence, even in a pocket cruiser: it is as much a part of your safety reserves as your lifejacket.

Arthur and Cheryl Bobstay are of that view, anyway. After a few years with a dinghy, they wanted to sail a bit further than the other bank of the reservoir, although they have no sights set on ambitious foreign trips or night crossings. The children are just of an age where sleeping overnight on a boat is their idea of fun, and so as long as the bunks are long enough to be able to stretch out and they can close up the cabin at night to keep out wind and rain, the Bobstays feel comfortable enough. It would have been nice to have had a boat with a lavatory that was hidden from general view, but they wanted to stay under 22ft and so that is one of the compromises they have had to make.

Poor old Arthur is a good six foot three tall, so there's no chance of him being able to stand up in the cabin of his 21ft *Wavedancer*; but even if he were of a more modest height, he would have to be thinking in terms of a 28-footer, not a pocket cruiser, before he could enjoy full standing headroom. As cruisers go, this one wasn't too hard on his pocket. It cost not much more than buying a decent car, and if he hadn't wanted to spend that much there was always the excellent second-hand market advertised over many pages of all the yachting magazines.

Cheryl has brought enough food aboard to last till Sunday teatime, which is the usual length of their cruise: off the mooring on Saturday morning, back by Sunday night. Moorings caused them a lot of worry. They couldn't afford the luxury of a marina berth, even though it would allow them to walk virtually straight from boat to car, so they've opted for a swinging mooring in the river. It is so called because the boat swings with the tide, moored by a rope over the bow which is in turn fastened to a heavy anchor buried deep in the mud on the river bed. Whether it's high or low tide, their boat will always be afloat. They did have the option of what is called a half-tide mooring. This means that for several hours a day, the boat will be high and dry, so until the tide returns you are either marooned aboard or ashore. It also means that you have to plan your cruises even more carefully, so as not to have a long wait if you arrive back home to find the tide has still several hours to rise before you can pick up the mooring. All in all, a half-tide mooring is a bit restricting, though usually quite cheap; so Arthur decided his all-tide mooring was money well spent. Instead, he economised on the tender, the small rowing boat that gets them from the shore to the mooring. This is always a false economy. There are more accidents through tenders capsizing than ever occur out at sea; he should have chosen something which is deep and stable, easy to row, not too heavy to launch, and light enough to tow behind his big boat on short trips. Many people find an inflatable (the Avons are among the most popular) the best solution; at least it can be deflated, rolled up and taken home at the end of every weekend.

Despite a damp row out to the boat, they are happy to be aboard and

Arthur has already started to unroll his charts. Wisely he chose a boat which at least had a solid surface on which he could navigate. The motion can be quite bouncy in a small cruiser and if navigation is difficult when the boat is still, it will be impossible when the weather turns against you. Which is precisely when good navigation matters most.

The children in the meantime are fighting over the bunks. As in most boats in this size range, there are two bunks towards the the front arranged in a 'V' shape filling the bow space, and two more down either side in the cabin. The bigger boats will have some kind of divider between the main cabin and the forepeak but the Bobstays make do with a curtain which they pull across when the children are asleep. Yes, they could sleep more if they wanted by putting a tent over the cockpit and sleeping two out there, but at times four seems more than enough for a boat of this size.

If the forecast is good, they might sail down the river till the estuary opens out, and then northwards towards a host of pretty harbours, none of them more than half a day's sail away. There's a two-burner cooker, so if it turns chilly they can have some hot soup on the way. And when they're safely at anchor for the night, they can work two-burner magic and rustle up a good cruising meal of beans and sausages. After supper, while the children are squeaking and giggling in the foc'sle behind the curtain, they read quietly in the cabin; at the moment they are seeking inspiration for a projected fair-weather dash to Holland by reading about some of the epic voyages that have been made in pocket cruisers, like David Blagden who took a 19-footer in the Transatlantic Race, or the 17-footer that rounded Cape Horn. A well-founded and well-sailed pocket cruiser might well turn out to be stronger than the people who cruise her. And with the thought in his mind that at least he has a boat which *might* take him to foreign parts, providing he has the inner strength, Arthur Bobstay slides into his sleeping bag. He bends his knees; if his little boat were only a foot longer, he would be able to stretch to his full length on his narrow bunk.

They awake the next morning to the sound of a gunshot. It cracks through the air and is quickly followed by shouted orders and the rasp of winches being wound at speed. Arthur stirs from his slumbers and sees through the tinted cabin window the usual sight of the local club racing fleet set off by the starter's gun, sprinting down the fairway for the first of the day's races. Hastily, he nips on deck to relieve himself before they get too close; the lavatory in his little boat is artfully concealed under the central plank of the foc'sle bunk, and the children are still fast asleep up there. He watches the fleet and is glad that when he was invited, he decided not to join Tom Luff's syndicate to buy a pocket racer. Horses for courses, he thinks; and happy in his miniature ship, he starts to fry the breakfast bacon on the little cooker, and puts on the kettle approximately eight inches from his sleeping wife's feet.

Tom Luff, leading the racing fleet downriver, is happy in his own way, too. He is inspired by the chase. He likes to test his skill against others, and since he hasn't got the money or time to mix it with the big boys down at Cowes, he relies on several deadly rivals here at the club, who have identical boats to his. When they race against each other, they can be certain that the first man home has sailed his boat the best.

Even though his syndicate's *Vindaloo* is no bigger than the Bobstays' boat, it is worlds apart in its equipment and the way it is sailed (it also cost more). There's a small spinnaker to think about, and a big light-weather ghosting jib; there are poles, sheets and guys to go with them; there is a device to alter the tension of the backstay (Arthur has to settle down for half-an-hour with the pliers for any such adjustment, and only does it once a year instead of three times a weekend); there are lines to control twist in the mainsail, and headsail sheeting angles to play with. That's why there's a crew of three or four for every race: when the boat is beating they sit in a neat row with their boots over the windward rail looking like a deputation from the Seven Dwarfs. Since they have no plans to spend a night aboard (unless Tom puts them aground on the mud again), not much attention is paid to the sleeping or cooking arrangements. All the bunks are full of sails and spare gear and tools. A bagful of 'nibbles' is depleted gradually through the day, the Mars Bars always going first and the health-food biscuits last. Tom's wife will have nothing to do with the boat.

His family aren't interested in sailing at all. If they had been, he might have compromised and bought what the salesmen call a cruiser-racer, so that he could go out with them sometimes, and beat up his mates at the club on the other weekends. He was quite relieved, in a way; he holds the view that cruiser-racers are the worst, rather than the best, of both worlds.

If you are thinking of a pocket racer, do ask around first to find out what other boats are being raced on the river or harbour where you intend to keep her. Imagine the frustration of buying a *Dagger 19*, only to find that they only race *Cut-Throat 22*s on your stretch of water. Of

course, most clubs have what's called a handicap class, in which the time you take to complete the course is adjusted according to an individual boat handicap rule that can vary from club to club. That way, anybody who feels like it can join in a race, even the Bobstays. But the keen, hard, racers tend to prefer strict class-racing. Less room for doubt when they do win!

Because the purpose-built racers are built to sail closer to the wind, they tend to be more 'tender' and heel more easily. That can make them wetter, especially as Tom Luff always carries as much sail as he dare in order to squeeze the last fraction of a knot out of his boat. Arthur Bobstay always reefs when the idea crosses his mind for the very first time; that way he's hardly ever caught out, and he spends more of his cruising upright. Tom Luff thinks Arthur is very boring; Arthur thinks Tom is mad. Horses for courses.

The Bobstays have their own little triumphs, though. This Sunday evening, they are pleased and smug to have judged their return just nicely: there's just enough water for them to be able to motor gently up to their mooring (it is an outboard motor incidentally, not enough room to waste on even the smallest petrol inboard. Arthur wouldn't want one, anyway; as long as an outboard is powerful enough, which it is, and well-stowed in a built-in well, he sees great advantages in having an engine he can take home and nurse through the winter).

Cheryl is just putting their mainsail-cover on when she catches sight of Pete and Pam Tiller. They're sliding a steel trailer down the concrete slipway, gently backing the car until the trailer is well submerged. If they judge it right this week, their boat *Pullalong* will float onto its trailer. After a certain amount of heaving and lashing and tying, Pete will drive cautiously forward and set off for home, like a tortoise with his home on his back.

There is much to be said for trailer-sailing. There is no problem with finding a permanent mooring, or the expense of renting one, since the boat lives most of the time in your garden. You can also cruise anywhere you wish provided you are prepared to tow your boat there. It can be Devon one weekend and Brighton the next. You will need a stout car, and expect to have to replace the clutch more often; and you'll have to get used to the trailer's speed limit. You'll also have to check the tides before you set off to ensure there's water on the slipway when you arrive. Whereas most of the big dayboats in the last chapter could, at a pinch, be manhandled in over the mud by four or six willing adults, the same is emphatically not true of a cruising boat with a deck and bunks and gear aboard.

Launching is a fine art. It looks easy, with the boat and trailer being gently eased into the water till the boat floats off of its own accord. But you then have to rig the mast, and all the sheets, and park the car and trailer; and if you've just had a five-hour drive, it is a tough start to a weekend. Recovery is even more complicated, especially if there's much wind or rough water. All the rigging has to be taken down and stowed securely for the road. And then the five-hour drive commences. On the other hand, at least when the September gales start to blow you know your boat is safe; you can see it out of the bedroom window. And you're not paying the boatyard to look after her, and because she's always around, you spend less of your valuable sailing time on maintenance. Trailer-folk like Bob and Pam never have the experience of driving miles on icy winter roads to do horrid little jobs with jammed seacocks, or service the lavatory; they do them in the evening, with power and light from their garage.

Ideally, there should be a boat that encompasses the virtues of the cruiser, the racer and the trailer-sailer. But the racer has to be fast, which would make the cruising less comfortable; the trailer-sailer has to be light, which can be a disadvantage out in a seaway; and the cruising boat has to be steady and comfortable below, which will slow her down and make her heavier. There are some wonderful boats on the market in this size; but it makes sense to get your priorities straight before you buy.

LITTLE SHIPS:

fit for Ramsgate or Rio

THE BORDERLINE BETWEEN 'pocket cruisers' and Little Ships is a difficult one to draw. Probably the safest way to express it is to say that a Little Ship is a yacht solid and seaworthy enough to take across the North Atlantic without drawing gasps of astonishment from onlookers. David Blagden took his tiny Hunter across, true; but that was a rare feat. Every year, hundreds of boats of 25 or 26ft overall length do the same trip, and are hardly noticed.

You may not, of course, want to go across the North Atlantic. But however unambitious a voyager you are, there is immense security to be had from the knowledge that the boat beneath you is one of a class that has gone through worse weather than you ever plan to be out in. In a blow off the West Coast of Ireland once, a friend of ours gasped, stumbling back from changing down to the storm jib, 'Don't worry – we're amateurs, but the boat's a professional!' It was a perfect express-ion of the way one comes to feel about a good boat; in a pocket cruiser or an open boat you are always conscious of the need to nurse the boat, and the duty not to let it face weather it wasn't meant for; in a little ship you can embark on a 72-hour open water passage (with a strong enough crew) and not be too uneasy about the fact that the weathermen can only guarantee moderate winds for the first 24 hours.

Take Francis Gunnell. His boat is fifteen years old, 27ft overall and 23ft on the waterline. Nobody has ever heard of him, and his colleagues at the Bank just know, vaguely, that he 'does a bit of sailing'. What they do not know is that from his home port of Poole he has covered 7000 miles a year on average, and that the reason he took four weeks of his annual leave in one slab last summer (greatly inconveniencing the Business Loans department) was that he had developed a yen to sail to Iceland. From Easter onwards, much helped by the spring succession of Bank Holidays, Francis worked his boat up weekend by weekend

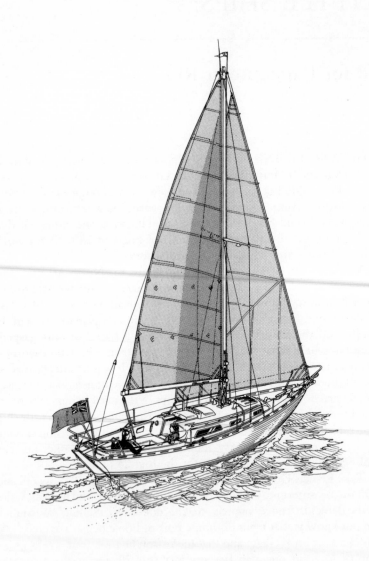

round the coast of Britain to Oban, on the West Coast of Scotland. Sometimes he took a friend, sometimes not; he sailed *Invicta* in anything except a firmly forecast gale of 8 or more. A headwind of Force 7 does not stop him setting out; even fifty miles up the coast was worth achieving in his three-day expeditions. Every Monday at dawn he was on some wretched milk-train, heading back for London, shaving as he went.

The effort paid off. By the time his holiday arrived he was in exactly the right place, with exactly the right weather-pattern – a gentle, steady summer Westerly – well-established. After a stop at the Faeroes, where he picked up a crew, an Icelander wanting a free trip home, he finally made it to Reykjavik. By which time it was nearly time to turn round, since the Bank Holidays thin out drastically in late summer, and he wanted to get farther south than Oban. In the event, assisted by his girlfriend who took a week's short-notice holiday and flew up to join him in the Faeroes, he got all the way back to Poole in twelve days with 2500 miles on the log. When he chugged into Poole Harbour, his friends in the marina – several with identical boats to his own – were boasting happily of their sixty-mile trips across to Normandy and the Channel Islands, and drinking up their duty-free.

Francis is no fool; he knows that when he and his girlfriend Susan marry, she will want shorter cruises, with longer spells spent ashore. He also knows that when they have children, Icelandic expeditions will cease for a few years, and he will be pretty grateful for their forbearance on a passage to Jersey or down to Benodet for some *frites* and a paddle on the beach. But even if he sells *Invicta*, and buys something with more bunks and a less rusty cooker as a gesture to family life, he will never buy a motorboat and he will never buy what he rudely terms a 'pisspot'. He has spent too long feeling the fierce and free sensation of a good boat beneath his feet, one that challenges every wave with gay good-humour, to descend to anything less.

When you choose a Little Ship you follow a lot of the same principles as before. But it makes sense to buy a member of a class of boats with a real voyaging pedigree. The smallest classic is the Folkboat, a seminal design from which several other famous boats have emerged, notably the Contessa 26. But there are a good many more modern designs which are equally tough and reliable.

There is no way that we could cover all the considerations you will have to make before buying such a serious boat. If this is your area, you

will certainly be reading magazines and books, and visiting Boat Shows and (if you are wise) insisting on trial sails before you buy anything. But here, to concentrate your mind, are the three basic things which make such a difference between one boat and another: hull form, rig, and accommodation.

There are dozens of fine points on hull design: broadly speaking, boats have got fatter and fatter in recent years, until they are almost shaped in plan like fat teardrops, instead of slender torpedoes. But the first thing to consider is the keel. The Folkboat family, for instance, small though they are at 26ft, are possessed of a traditional full keel. Now long-keeled boats are heavy; they are not going to fly along in light winds; but they have the inestimable advantage of being steady. That great weight of lead beneath them makes them move more gently than a lighter boat; you may find they make you less sick in a choppy sea than their lighter, modern cousins. Also, a boat with a full keel has great directional stability. This, in layman's terms, means that you can take your hand off the tiller to scratch your nose or stir your tea, and the boat will continue to thump on regardless for a minute or two before rounding up into the wind. A boat with a small narrow 'fin' keel and a tiny skeg to protect the rudder, especially if it is otherwise very flat-bottomed, will spin round like a top the moment it stops feeling a firm hand on the tiller. It is the difference between driving a steady plough-horse and riding a skittish show-jumper. To be fair, the performance reflects the same difference; a long-keeled boat is not going to accelerate rapidly in every puff of wind either. There are, of course, compromises; some fin keels are so substantial they almost behave like full keels. Another thing to consider is whether you plan to 'take the ground' often; that is, to dry out alongside a harbour wall at low tide. The longer your keel's base is, the safe you will be doing this. If you want to dry out and not bother with a wall at all, you either need the very traditional combination of a good big keel and removable 'legs' to put down, or else a 'bilge-keel' boat, with two slightly splayed out keels, one either side just on the turn of the bilge. There are plenty of bilge keelers around; they used to be frequently slandered by single-keelers who said they were bad at sailing to windward; frankly, with the newer designs there is no proof of this at all. Finally on this subject, think hard before you commit yourself to something advertised as a 'motor-sailer'. There are motorboats – some very fine ones – with motorboaty wheelhouses and powerful engines, which have masts but

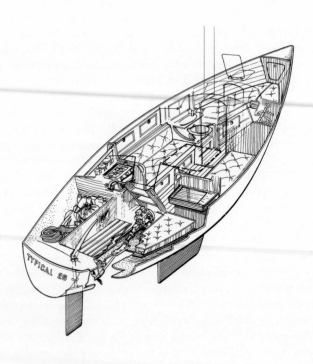

barely sail at all unless the wind is very fair and very brisk. If that is what you want, they will do you well. but if you really want to sail, and are just hoping for a bit of extra 'insurance' in the motor department, you really might do as well with one of the real sailing-boats which just have a good diesel engine. Modern marine diesels are excellent; there are many easily driven hulls on the market; and nothing is more disappointing than to be stuck with a great wallowing lump of motorboat when, in almost equal comfort, you could be quietly sailing with the same wind. The next thing to think about is rig. Ten years ago, this would not have been much of a problem; with a small yacht at least, what you got was standard Bermudan rig, the one children draw in their school exercise books: two triangles either side of a mast. Most boats are still Bermudan-rigged, with various refinements like roller reefing headsails to save much work on the foredeck, and stow-away mainsails which actually roll up inside the mast. But there are other options, and if you are buying a new boat, it is worth thinking about, or testing, such exotic options as Junk Rig (Chinese style, one sail only, very easy to reef – never scoff at it, Blondie Hasler and Michael Richey have persistently sailed the famous Folkboat *Jester* in the gruelling Observer Singlehanded Transatlantic Race under junk rig); Cat Rig, which is disturbingly like a giant sailboard, with a wishbone, in appearance, and includes an equally disturbing unstayed mast (but don't scoff at that, either; the famous Freedom boats have proved its worth); and Gaff (Cutter) Rig, now making a surprising, but gratifying, comeback. It is popular with people who like a pretty, traditional outline and appreciate having two small foresails instead of one socking great one which is heavy to haul in (you can, of course, have a Bermudan cutter and reap this same benefit). Another thing to look at when considering the rig is whether this boat has been designed and laid out for shorthanded sailing or for labour-intensive racing. It is possible for the same operation aboard two boats of the same size to need one hand or six; and it is not only singlehanders who need ease on deck. If you sail with a family of youngish children, or frequently take landlubbing friends away for the weekend, believe me, you count as shorthanded. One Irish yacht charter skipper described his day-trips with visitors out to see the island view as 'singlehanding, but with an obstacle course in the way'. If you plan to race, or always to have a strong crew, you can afford a more complicated, labour-intensive rig.

The third matter is accommodation. While you can, in theory, virtually rebuild most boats inside, it will cost you a lot of money. So if you heartily dislike the atmosphere and accommodation of your prospective cabin, for heaven's sake don't buy it. We once spent two years painstakingly trimming acres of austere Formica with wooden beading and screwing brass lamps onto it to soften its harsh appearance, and in the end gave up and sold the boat. If the boat has not got enough bunks or not enough workspace in the galley, or no proper chart table, think hard before falling in love with it. You may not live permanently on your boat, but the bits of your life you *do* lead aboard will be far more intense than ashore; if it is the wrong sort of home for you, it will irritate you disproportionately; if it is a comfortable and well-ordered place, you will not only be happier, but safer too.

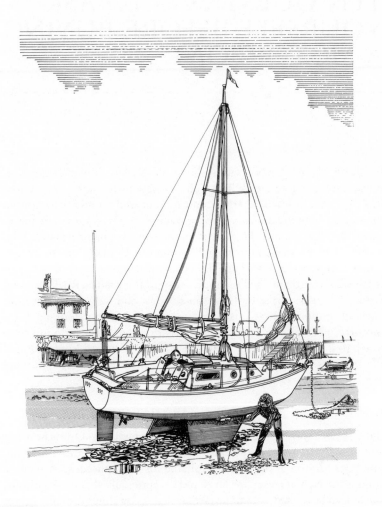

TEN QUESTIONS TO ASK YOURSELF BEFORE BUYING A MOTORBOAT

PEOPLE WHO WANT sailing-boats are always, however unambitious, embracing a new skill as well as a new possession. They know that they have to learn the ropes, and are prepared for odd behaviour in their craft, such as suddenly leaning over at 45 degrees, or refusing to travel directly upwind. They are also, by their very nature, people who reckon that the main pleasure will come out of being on the water, rather than getting anywhere. Indeed, ocean-racers carry this to unreasonable lengths by sailing all the way to the Fastnet Rock, passing within five mile of the best pubs in Europe, and sailing straight back without stopping. It is possible, however, to go out looking for a motorboat for a variety of quite different reasons, which do not have much to do with the water. Without wishing to be insulting (some of the attitudes below are actually ours, as well) we offer the following exercise in self-examination:

1. DO I REALLY JUST WANT A CAR THAT GOES ON WATER?

If the answer is 'yes', then there are two considerations. One is how big and powerful a waterborne car to get; the other is whether the 'road' you plan to drive it on is really suitable for this approach. A canal, a sluggish stretch of river, or a large and exceptionally sheltered harbour, can indeed be treated not unlike tarmacadam: you chug from one side of it to the other, your principal concern being to get from A to B without bumping into a fellow-traveller. Even so, you have to be aware that engine failure may well leave you with no means of getting anywhere at all. And if you run out of petrol, you can't walk to the nearest filling-station.

If you really mean 'yes' to this question, and are genuinely unwilling to learn anything about boat-handling and the treacherous ways of water, you are not altogether a safe person to go boating with – even without any possibility of being blown or carried out into open water. Even the middle of the fast-flowing River Thames, or the calm sea 100 yards off Hastings beach, counts as open water for this purpose.

2. AM I BASICALLY LOOKING FOR TRANSPORT?

If being on the water is not an end in itself, but a means of fishing, getting to islands for picnics, etc., then a motorboat will do you nicely, and you can start to consider size. At the humbler end of the market, you can put an outboard on almost anything – even your steady little sailing dinghy, with her canvas down – and it will do the job. Small outboards, however, are not to be trusted with your life against a fast tide or strong wind; nor can you rely on even the most brilliant mechanic in the crew being able to fix them in a choppy sea and an offshore wind, with one wet spark-plug and the wrong size of plug-spanner. If you intend to go anywhere where you couldn't easily row ashore, take local advice on what size of engine is going to be man enough for the job. Which leads to:

3. AM I PLANNING TO GO TO SEA?

The ground-rule here is not to get involved with waves unless you have a boat with a seagoing profile – that is, reasonable ballast below the waterline, probably some sort of V-shape as opposed to a flat bottom; and to have 'positive buoyancy' – ie something which will float if you get swamped. This could mean anything from a sturdy open boat like the professional beach-fishermen use, with a good outboard, to a small cabin cruiser. But do not necessarily assume that your four-berth, luxury cabin cruiser from the Broads or other inland waterways is suitable for use at sea. It may be; but talk to the boatyard when you buy it, and be frank about your intentions.

4. DO I REALLY WANT TO SPEND NIGHTS ABOARD?

Not a silly question. Quite a few people, who really just want to fish and potter, waste money on boats with bunks and never sleep in them. There are some charming little motorboats around, much cheaper, which just have little cuddies for shelter and a one-burner stove for

making tea. The space saved can provide more room for fishing tackle and slimy buckets.

5. DO I WANT TO MAKE REAL VOYAGES?

If so, you need to apply to your motor-yacht the same rigorous conditions – and the same research – that you would have spent on your Little Ship in the sailing-boat section of this book. Twin engines are a great safety feature; so are decent cooking and sleeping arrangements – fatigue strikes motor-yachtsmen as much as sailors – and a comfortable, workmanlike navigation area. You will definitely need navigation classes if you want to make passages out of sight of land; even coastal trips are safer with a bit of basic training or reading behind you. And try to get some idea of how your prospective boat will actually behave in a big beam sea – that is, one where the waves roll inexorably at you from one side; sailing-boats, because of their ballast and the way the sails themselves hold them steady, are often a lot pleasanter at sea than a motorboat that rolls like the proverbial pig.

6. DO I WANT A MOTORBOAT BECAUSE SAILING SOUNDS TOO MUCH BOTHER?

Hundreds of people every year buy motorboats because they want to get afloat, but are shy of sailing schools and yacht clubs and the whole mystique of sailing. Sometimes it is only a few months later that they sell their motorboat (at a loss) and buy something with a mast. We hope this book has done something to demystify matters; but there is still a quite understandable feeling that if you have never had a boat, and want to be rapidly the master of your own ship, the short-cut is to avoid sails. It is not by any means the main reason people buy motor cruisers in areas where they could be sailing – you don't have to like sails in order to like the water – but it is definitely a strong one. All we would say is: Think carefully. It might be that you could buy a small sailing cruiser with a reliable engine, motor around for a few months, then one day decide to add a new dimension to your boating by cautiously hauling up the mainsail and seeing what happens . . .

7. AM I A SPEED FREAK?

If so, be honest about it and buy a speedboat, with the sort of hull expressly designed to streak over the water. Trying to drive a heavy displacement boat always at its maximum speed will not do either of you any good. Get a ski-boat or speedboat, and have fun. But don't expect it to be fit for a potter up the canals; fast boats are notoriously difficult to control at low speeds, that is beneath 10 knots.

8. DO I REALLY WANT A COUNTRY COTTAGE, ONLY ON WATER?

Perfectly sound reason for getting a boat, only again, face up to it. If you are going to confine yourself happily to the Broads, or other inland waterways, or to the interior of a big estuarial harbour, you can afford to consider comfort first, engine-power second. Comfort can reach great heights in big motor-yachts; you can have a corner bath if you want . . . or a jacuzzi. Since water is still water, however, do equip your country cottage with an anchor and sufficient chain, lifejackets, emergency flares and a dinghy in which you can row ashore with a diesel can or two, should you end up drifting around helplessly. Even in Barton Broad.

9. DO I WANT A STATUS SYMBOL?

Not such a good reason. If you really love boats, they are fun, stimulating, relaxing, and profoundly satisfying. If you don't, they may turn out to be frightening, boring, and exhausting. If you just want to feel like Charles Frere in *Howard's Way*, relaxing with a corseted floosie aboard a million-quid gin palace, make sure you can afford that ultimate rich man's bit of boating equipment – a professional skipper. Otherwise, although the Boating Industry will not much like our saying this, you might be better off with a Porsche . . .

10. DO I SECRETLY WANT TO BE JACK HAWKINS IN *THE CRUEL SEA*?

Absolutely no problem. There are some wonderfully 'shippy' looking motor-yachts and motor-sailers around, new or second-hand; many of them have traditional ventilators, brass-and-varnished wheels, lighted binnacles and even (I swear, I saw it at the 1984 Boat Show) speaking-tubes to bark orders into, if anyone should be listening below. Every man's, or woman's, most romantic fantasy can be fulfilled by some section of our humming boat industry. Our only reservation would be that if you start by wanting to be Jack Hawkins, you may well be wanting to be Charles Laughton in *Mutiny on the Bounty* after a few more months; in which case, make it a motor-sailer. Then you can cram on canvas when the mood takes you, and shout 'Mr Christian, damn you – carry on or carry under!'

MEETING THE FOLKS:

clubs and chaps

IT IS NOT LIKE golf, where you have to be a member of a club before they'll let you anywhere near the greens: if you simply want to go on the water, you needn't belong to anything at all. With the exception of one or two reservoirs where the water authority has granted a particular club sole sailing rights, you can launch, sail away and cock a snook at flags and flag officers. An Englishman's boat is his castle. But you might be missing a lot, not only in hot showers, bar food and comradeship, but in the wealth of experience and local knowledge that is often to be found tucked away at the end of a bar behind a pint glass that is always in need of a refill. Clubs are worth thinking about, at least when you first go on the water.

NATIONAL CLUBS

Perhaps we should start with the national associations. The one club which offers no premises and little comradeship is, in fact, possibly the most important of the lot: the Royal Yachting Association, or RYA. Do not be fooled by the title: clubs with the 'Royal' preface are usually as difficult to get into as a tin of sardines, but the RYA is open to all comers on the production of a modest cheque. It is the nearest thing there is to an official national representative body for all the motley collection of boat people in Britain. They use your money to administer excellent training schemes and award certificates to all classes of sailors, from dinghy beginners to ocean-going yachtmasters. They also represent the views of yachtsmen to the relevant Government departments and lobby on your behalf if they feel the sport is being restricted in any way. If you are a member of the RYA and want to influence the way it is run, or the balance it holds between cruising and racing, it is open to you to do so. There is a flag to fly, a regular newspaper and attractive insurance schemes.

Also throwing its arms wide open to members from any part of the country is the Cruising Association. If you want to sail around the coast of Britain or Western Europe, not being a member of this club would be like setting off with an arm tied behind your back. It is first and foremost an information source on all aspects of cruising. It has a vast collection of fully corrected charts that are available for all members to inspect, and beneath the low, arched brickwork of its clubhouse by the side of Tower Bridge, you can while away the winter months poring over charts and pilot books and planning your cruise for the next season. The library is better than any other that is readily available to sailors, and has a fine view of Thames Barges and massive yachts from every window. There can hardly be a club which offers its members a more inspiring setting. Many provincial sailors come to London in the winter months to spend a few peaceful days among the books and charts; Londoners find the place a magnet. Afloat, the club comes into its own not only through the famous Cruising Association Handbook, a pilot book giving navigational details of every nook and cranny in Europe, but through its network of CA Boatmen. The boatmen network is a sort of cruising man's RAC: they are listed in the CA's annual year book together with the harbour in which they can be found and the facilities they have available: engine spares, craneage, slipway etc. There is one in every major harbour in Britain and if you have a problem, he is a good first point of reference. As a service, it works well. We were stuck on the wild West Coast of Ireland with a seized engine and made a phone call to the CA Boatman a few miles away. He was with us within half an hour and brought life back to our motor with no more than a few blows of his hammer. It worked without fail for two years after that!

The Cruising Association is also an educational establishment and like its close neighbour, the Little Ship Club, it offers lectures and talks throughout the winter months not only at its headquarters but also through the many regional branches. There is bound to be one near you.

If you are only thinking of sailing and would like to try it before parting with any serious money, then a subscription to the Island Cruising Club would be money well spent. They have a floating clubhouse, *Egremont*. She is a converted Mersey Ferry and now rests at the top of Salcombe Harbour and provides cabins, canteens and a base for a fleet of seven magnificent cruising yachts from sloops to schooners, as well as being mother-ship to fleet of both modern and traditional dinghies. The atmosphere is rough and ready (no room service aboard *Egremont*); it is well organised and welcomes all ages. A week with the ICC is a perfect way of coming face to face with what sailing is all about.

If you already own a boat it might be worth asking the builders if there is a class association. If it's a racing dinghy there certainly will be but if it is a production cruiser, you're less likely to find one, largely because class associations tend to concern themselves mostly with laying down class rules for racing and running national championships. But a cruiser-owners association can be a mine of good information if your boat happens to be of a class that has spawned one. If you find that you can't change the fanbelt on the engine without having to remove the keel, or that one of the lockers persistently fills with bilgewater on the starboard tack, you can bet that you won't be the first owner to have discovered the problems; and within the pages of the association newsletter you're more than likely to find the answers to questions which have kept you awake in the long winter nights.

LOCAL CLUBS

It is surprising how many people who are new to the water feel that they must belong to the yacht club whose dining-room window looks out on the stretch of water on which they want to sail. Unless you want to make friends with the people there, or unless they have some facility which would make life a lot easier for you, then there is hardly any point in joining. I sailed for many years on the East Coast without ever being a member of anything and at the end of every weekend I just hauled the dinghy up the muddy slipway into the boatyard, fell into the car and drove home, smelly and salt-sore. It was only when I discovered that the local yacht club had showers and that their flashy new floating pontoon meant I wouldn't have to make any more of those muddy pilgrimages up the slippery slipway, that I set about joining. I was a member for quite a few years and never used any facility other than the washroom and the dinghy park but there again, there were a considerable number of members who never used anything but the dining room and the bar. It is by achieving such a balanced mix of members that clubs are able to survive.

Joining clubs is not always easy, and the more 'Royal' they like to

appear and the more like fortresses their clubhouses look, the more difficult it will be to get in. You will have to be proposed and seconded and if you are joining the club with the intention of making friends, it is difficult to see how you can find sponsors, because you haven't made any friends yet. Solve the paradox by going to see the secretary and if he treats you like scum, the club's not worth joining anyway.

You can't generalize about Yacht Clubs. Some are pompous, some are free-and-easy; some are cliquey (if you don't own a Finn, drop dead) and some are genuinely friendly. Some welcome families with children, others hate them. Some have strong roots in the local community, some are entirely made up of weekenders. All we can do is to paint for you the portrait of two extremes: and let you feel your way, cautiously, into a decent club which strikes the balance that you and your family want.

The Royal St Antony Mud Lump Yacht Club (R.StA.M.L.Y.C., founded 1888) Come in. Wipe your feet, and enter the granite portals of the Royal Mud Lump YC, pausing to admire the picture-window over the harbour and the spotless white flagpole. Here is Brigadier Sir Rodney Cummerbund-Flush, the Commodore. He is sitting in a huge leather armchair in the bar, under an improbable painting of a Napoleonic man o'war under full sail surrounded by two inches of rococo gilding. With him is the whippet-thin, bespectacled, hopelessly chinless figure of the Secretary. The Commodore is barking at the Secretary about a race programme. From the bar itself come faint, intimidating 'Haw haw haw' sounds. It is very cold. Enter a recent member, Arthur Winch. He finds it all a bit daunting, but he joined in the first place because the club has a noble history and is one of the pillars of the yachting establishment. Arthur's also heard that the club claret is a drop o'good. The Treasurer, a stout property-developer who likes to pretend he has Admirals in the family somewhere, once rendered Arthur speechless with shame by gazing into the back of his old Cavalier at a crate of Sainsbury's plonk, and sniffing 'False economy old boy. It always pays to *buy good.*'

Arthur agreed cravenly, instead of bravely pointing out that since the club sub. is nearly £300 a year, and the entrance fee was the same again, he is left with little to spend on liquid refreshment. Then there's the Mess dress. Never having been in the services, Arthur finds this a new concept; he does not relish the prospect of another £300 for a Saville

Row mess suit which might only be seen on two occasions a year, the Fitting Out Dinner and the Laying Up Dinner (Tickets £15 a head, prawn cocktail, pork chop, Duchesse potatoes and trifle). He is hesitating, though; he vainly thinks it might enhance his status in the club. His wife, however, has expressed the view that the tightly-buttoned bumfreezer jacket would only make him look like a stuffed duck.

He may not be entirely easy in club company yet, but having joined, he is at least part of a network of clubs offering reciprocal hospitality. He can therefore sail as far away as Sydney or Salcombe and find clubs that will welcome him as if he were a long-lost brother. They are all listed in the rulebook (which also sets out the fines that members are likely to incur if they should happen to tear the baize on the billiard table).

The only nagging fear that Arthur has is that this is not, secretly, a sailing club at all. Yacht club yes; sailing club, no. There is a boot boy who will give your hand-made shoes a quick rub over, but don't expect him to handle muddy sailing wellies. In the cloakroom, you're more likely to find tailoring by Burberry than Henri-Lloyd. Members arriving bedraggled and heroic from an Atlantic crossing will not be welcome in the Bar until they have changed into reefer-jackets. Besides, the last four fellow-members he plucked up the courage to speak to were owners either of no boat at all, or of huge gin-palaces dedicated to carrying crumpet to Cowes for the weekend, and back again. Still, his membership is looked on with envy by his non-boating friends, and the Royal in the title allows him the simple daydream that one day, he might come out of the marble-floored Gents and run into the Princess of Wales . . . Just as such thoughts are crossing his mind, Commodore Cummerbund-Flush lumbers across. Poor old Arthur. Someone saw him on the Solent last weekend flying a blue ensign with the Royal Mud Lump burgee and his blue ensign warrant will not be through for another week, not officially . . . Oh dear. If only Arthur had been to public school, he might understand it all a bit better.

Bumblesea Sailing Club (B.S.C., founded 1955, we think, only the Secretary has lost the original document). It may look like an unlovely overgrown public loo, but Bumblesea SC is made out of the best-loved, most sweated-over breezeblocks in the country. The members, after humble beginnings in a Portacabin, built most of the club themselves, and raised the money for the rest. The swing doors are propped open; anyone can squelch in from the sea, although the committee have been trying to bring in a rule about no wetsuits in the bar for five years now. The motion is always blocked by the younger element. There is a huge, echoing cloakroom with a good many rusty lockers and plenty of pegs; at the moment it is full of small children, arguing shrilly about racing rules. The Optimist and Mirror classes are busy this weekend. In the bar, their parents are sitting around, some on tea-chests upholstered with leftover foam from someone's home-completed yacht, drinking very good draught beer. There are no leather armchairs and no Commodore in sight. The duty barman, a member, has gone off to sort out his son's Mirror, which has come drastically unrigged for some reason, so everyone is pulling their own pints and leaving money in an untidy, beery pile on the bar. Enter Stan and Betty Forestay, who want to be members. They are bought a drink, the Secretary is found, and they explain what their boat is. The Secretary thinks it may take a week or two, but insists they use the club meanwhile. The club also intends to use them: Stan, a muscular chap, finds himself mysteriously co-opted to spend next weekend helping to lay some new club moorings, even though he has a trailer boat and doesn't need one. While he is out on the old landing-craft the club uses for its mooring-work ('We don't believe in paying good money to contractors, old boy'), Betty is buttering sandwiches for a visiting fleet's tea ('We don't believe in paying caterers, old girl'). Young Jimmy Forestay, however, has struck lucky; he is going to crew someone's dinghy for the afternoon, and has even been lent a buoyancy aid. Within three weekends, the family have settled down as Bumblesea members; they have their own burgee (the BSC burgee is enormous and garishly coloured, so that members can recognize one another in foreign ports and raft up together for a festive evening) and their own slot in the dinghy-rack. They never intended to race their little boat, but have been signed on for two cruiser-races by the indefatigable Martin, the club beaver ('That's the spirit, that's the spirit'). Most important of all, they are starting to look forward to seeing the familiar faces dragging their dinghies to the water every weekend. The subscription is £15 a year, £17 for families.

Most clubs lie somewhere between the two. *Caveat emptor.*
(See Appendix I.)

LEARNING THE ROPES:

courses, wet and dry

IF YOUR PROPOSED boat is not much more than a car on water, if you do not mean to go into tidal waters, do not intend to hoist sails or row, and propose to solve any mechanical breakdown problem by stepping smartly onto the nearest bank and walking to a garage, then you do not need to take a course. Skip this chapter, and use the time practising breast-stroke (the only skill every single boat user needs) up and down the local baths.

But if you mean to confront the sea, to sail and navigate and plan voyages; if you want to be 'seamanlike' – which is merely a maritime term covering efficiency and prudence – then you may well need to take some kind of instruction. If you live in Britain, there is not much point having anything to do with any instructor or school not approved and affiliated to the Royal Yachting Association, the RYA. They are the benchmark; they have their own syllabuses for various degrees of competence, publish textbooks, and even conduct examinations for the loftiest qualification of all, the Yachtmaster. There is an Appendix to this book which sets out the contents of the courses and should give you an idea of where to aim. However, even RYA-approved courses and instructors vary widely in their aims and methods; so here are some types:

THE PRACTICAL DINGHY SCHOOL

No-nonsense, tough and enthusiastic young instructors take trainees out in dinghies, and give shore instruction on the principles of sailing, safety, racing rules (if you want), and basic seamanship and knots. They are famous for going out, within sheltered waters, in the foulest weather, so it is most unlikely you will waste your money. Children and teenagers seem to adore these courses, especially out of their

71

parents' sight; the least enthusiastic trainees are those in middle-age who 'feel silly', and resent being ordered about by a tanned 22-year-old in a designer wetsuit. Such people are best off taking one or two basic lessons, then learning, cautiously, to potter around on their own.

THE PRACTICAL YACHT SCHOOL, OR 'WET' COASTAL/ YACHTMASTER COURSE

Some instruction in cruising yachts is very like a dinghy course – that is, you go out for the day and come back at night to sleep in a hotel or some sort of budget barracks. But you will never get the real feel of yacht cruising that way; a far better bet is to go for one of the schools which actually takes you away for a week, or even a fortnight, on a real voyage. What happens is that you join up, nervously clutching your floppy sailing bag (the mark of a real tyro is bringing a suitcase – you can't stow them on yachts!), and find you are on a roomy cruiser with perhaps five other pupils and a skipper-instructor. After a brief shakedown sail, in which you learn which bits of the boat are which, you will probably be divided up into watches, with each pair (or, sometimes, individual) totally in charge of planning and conducting one leg of the voyage. Skipper, of course, is watching; we greatly admired the iron nerve of one who managed to stay in his bunk all night, with one beady eye opening occasionally and the odd surreptitious glance at the chart, while Libby navigated home from Wexford to Wales in a following Force 8 gale. Shrill little squeaks of 'Is it flashing three, Dave? or four? no, really, it matters – it has to be three or it isn't the right lighthouse, I think, hang on, there's cocoa on the chart –' utterly failed to bring this heroic man up on deck to take over. It was the right light, and we got in at dawn feeling like Christopher Columbus; it was a fast and effective way to learn responsibility. However, ambitious courses like these are most useful if you have already done the 'dry' navigation course (*qv*), and learned the basics.

THE NAVIGATION EVENING CLASS

There is something faintly ridiculous about leaning out of a classroom window in a College of Further Education in Oxfordshire, and solemnly taking a moon-sight which, after an hour's laborious calculation, places you somewhere East of Suez (must have turned two pages over somewhere). But local authority evening classes are actually a fine way to pass the winter learning something which will be inestimably useful to you in the summer. There you sit, back in the classroom with your books and exercise-sheets, pencils sharpened, mind struggling rustily back into action after years out of school; and you learn a new skill. Navigation, especially coastal navigation, is not as daunting as it sounds; it is 20 per cent rote-learning (remembering what buoys look like and chart symbols mean), 10 per cent arithmetic (not even mathematics) and 70 per cent sheer applied commonsense. The commonsense aspect is most important: it has been known for a pupil to get home on the first night from class, and laboriously lay off a proposed course across a clean homework practice-chart, only to have an interested flatmate lean over and say 'Oh, isn't that a sandbank you've gone through?' The reply, on this occasion, was 'Well, it might be. We haven't *done* sandbanks yet'. It is better to make these mistakes in your living-room than in the Thames Estuary. A good instructor can make it all come alive, even in his landlocked classroom on a January night, and you will be glad of him when you first take your boat to sea.

Incidentally, on no account confuse 'Coastal Navigation' with 'Astro-Navigation' on the college noticeboard. Astro-Navigation is fascinating, useful if you go far offshore, and perfectly easy for even a non-mathematician to assimilate with a bit of concentration; but it is most definitely Stage Two stuff. If you are just starting to sail, and plan to go no farther than the next harbour along the coast, you need the Coastal skills first – tides, buoyage, dead-reckoning, taking fixes. You do not need to be dazzled and confused by the arcana of noon-sights and moon-sights, not yet anyway.

THE CORRESPONDENCE COURSE

If there is no local course, or you are the type who works better alone, you can do all the Coastal skills – up to Yachtmaster theoretical level – by post. Astro-Navigation is also available by post, and quite popular: Paul actually learned his this way, and reports:

'It was only the meanness that I inherited through my Yorkshire bloodline that made me stick at my astro correspondence course. I had paid a hundred quid, so I went the full distance. Every month for a year, a trigonometrically intricate package of teaching material, graph paper and test questions would thud onto the doormat, and I would know that at least three evenings of that week were going to be fully occupied with movement of the heavenly bodies. I have to say it was far easier than moving my own heavenly body down the road to the technical college; if, like me, you are the victim of an unpredictable work pattern, a correspondence course is a good solution. But you must have stamina or meanness enough to get you through it!

I had not chosen the most suitable course. It was advanced astro, and by lesson six I could do all the corrections for sights taken near the equator, and allow for problems at both North and South poles. All I actually wanted to be able to do was get the plastic sextant out of its box somewhere between the Needles and Cherbourg and get a rough idea of where I was. I never thought I would have to get to grips with the spherical triangle. I have since learnt that a classic book by Mary Blewitt would have told me all I needed to know, and would have taken roughly a tenth of the time to understand. However, if I ever have to swing a sextant in anger, I shall be able to do so. I keep in practice by taking at least two or three sights every cruise. The first one usually takes a good half hour and much cursing, and gives us a position somewhere in the correct hemisphere. By the third, it's much smoother, and I begin to believe that the intellectual sweat of the correspondence course was well worth it. Like bicycle-riding, once learned it is difficult to forget'.

There's no way that a through-the-post system can ever teach you the feel of the wind or the weather or when it's time to reef, but for theoretical knowledge of flags and knots, running fixes and tidal calculations, it's as good as any other teaching method for people who can muster the necessary concentration. However, you can have a considerably jollier time in a small evening class with a nice instructor (like Libby's, who used to shout 'Near enough for Nellie, Near enough for Nelson' whenever she was less than two miles out in her answer), and you can all go down to the pub afterwards and tell one another improbable tales of your last summer's exploits.

There are two other ways to learn seamanship and navigation:

JUST READING BOOKS

You can, of course, learn anything you need to know from a book. Up to a point. There is no sailing subject on which a good book has not been written. Many of our earlier voyages were conducted tiller in one hand, open book in the other. (Publishers please take note, use stronger binding, and put the chapter on reefing earlier on, please). The only guide to good books is yourself: browse in a chandlery, and only buy the ones which seem 'user-friendly', and have clear illustrations. And have nothing to do with an 'action' book which doesn't have an index. When your spouse is on the helm, in the dark, in a shipping-lane, babbling something about three red lights and one white, or is it two red lights one above the other and a green light, you want an index with the words *LIGHTS, NAVIGATION, recognition of.* If it is a pair-trawler dragging a net towards your keel, you might as well know . . .

LEARNING FROM YOUR HUSBAND/WIFE/BOYFRIEND/ GIRLFRIEND

Almost always hopeless. Especially if it is the woman who is learning, and the man is not all that experienced himself. Once the fatal words 'For heavens' sake, woman . . .' have crossed his lips, the enterprise is doomed. Most people are far better off learning the basics from an instructor, either alongside or (even better) away from their partner.

GETTING THE GEAR:

the chandlery panic

THERE IS ALMOST no limit to what you can spend on boating equipment. Walk into any big chandlery and you will be dazzled by gadgetry, ravished by new shades and patterns of waterproof, and alarmed by the huge variety of safety equipment you can't possibly afford. Television programmes like *Howard's Way* give the impression that it is positively unwise to go afloat without everything gleaming new, and the whole crew in matching pearl-grey and pink designer oilskins. If you are new to boating, and suffering from a slight sense of inferiority after tangling your rigging up in the davits of a moored gin-palace and running yourself aground, you may feel like compensating for all this by recklessly waving a credit card around.

Depending on your credit, this may or may not be a good idea. There is some marvellous gear around: whether you are talking about satellite navigation systems or stretchy protective socks to put round your fenders, you will find it easily accessible on the shelves. Gone are the days (some say, alas) when a chandler was just someone who sold you a coil of rope, a can of paraffin, and a spare shackle-pin. Chandlery now is big consumer buiness, and has learned all the wiles of the modern marketplace. Some pieces of perfectly ordinary equipment – echo-sounders, jamming-cleats, paintstripper – are now packaged so seductively that they arouse something close to lust. What chance have we, wet and weary and longing for comfort, against the siren song of 'specially imported' Scandinavian anti-condensation thermal under-suits, or miraculous substances that promise to remove suntan oil from sailcloth? If you are a traditionalist, there are racks of beautiful shiny new fids to tempt you; if you suffer from the modern disease of techno-lust, you will be salivating helplessly in front of a display of Yachtsmen's Cellular Telephones, or held mesmerized by that haunting, expensive word, *Decca*.

But take a deep breath, step outside, and look at your boat again, and the brown water it bobs on. You don't need half this stuff. Correction: you don't need a quarter of it, even if you have a bare 30ft hull to fit out. Some of it will bring pleasure, some a margin of extra security; but you can do without what you can't afford.

Let us take safety first. I would not use the word 'blackmail', but some advertising of marine safety gear makes it a tempting one. The trouble is that there will *always* be something new which – in extreme circumstances of the right kind – might save your life. It could be a collision-damage repair system, or a miniature self-inflating liferaft attached to a Dan-buoy, or an exceptionally powerful radio for signalling your position to aircraft. All these are perfectly good pieces of equipment; if you can afford them they may help you and will certainly give you extra confidence; but if you can't afford them, should you feel guilty?

Probably not. There are certain irreducible necessities: any boat that goes outside a harbour should have distress flares, a fire extinguisher and lifejackets. For real cruising, there should always be a dinghy (if not liferaft) which is accessible, and perhaps a VHF radio for distress calls. If there is a cooker, there should be a fire-blanket. And so on: it is all pretty much a matter of commonsense. The RYA publish recommended lists; if you want a very comprehensive safety invoice, the Royal Ocean Racing Club recommendations can't be bettered. Beyond that, what generally happens is that people provide for their own pet fears – fire, holing, dismasting or whatever – and for the eventuality they think is most likely. For instance, many yachts carry wire-cutters in case of a dismasting, to get rid of the mast before it knocks a hole in the boat.

Next, clothing. Again, it is tempting to equip yourself from the skin outward in some manufacturer's pet 'system' – moisture-wicking underclothes, etc. And some of them are very good indeed, even on the most taxing ocean-race. On the other hand, as Michael Green immortally put in the *The Art of Coarse Cruising*, a Coarse yachtsman can be recognized by his clothes, which are a set of leftovers 'from other sports he has failed at': mountaineering anoraks, motorbike overtrousrs, athletics singlets etc. Both approaches are permissible. It is certainly a great thing to have one decent heavy-weather oilskin jacket, with velcro at the wrists, a really waterproof hood, and a built-in harness attachment point: it makes you feel tougher and more confident straight away. But even these last for years and years, properly cared for; there is no reason whatsoever for replacing it with the latest, slightly fancier model every other year. As for basic clothes, any normal outdoor casual wear will do: sweaters are best in wool, but don't need to be blue; fabrics like polyester are best avoided, because they hold so little warmth, but ordinary loose cotton trousers are ideal. Denim jeans are the only common outdoor-wear to be avoided like the plague; they are too tight, and too thick. Once they get damp saltiness into them, they will cling horribly, and never dry out until thoroughly washed. Looser, thin but tough cotton trousers in blue or that curious yachtsmen's pink are cheaply available in most chandleries. As for shoes, although the trend is towards leather deck-shoes, which are durable and wonderfully comfortable, if you are broke you can happily compromise on canvas ones, and throw away one pair a season. You need a woolly hat, but it doesn't have to be a specially imported Breton knit; you need boots, but they don't have to be smart yellow wellies. The short black-and-white 'pint of porter' boots are perfectly adequate, especially with oilskin trousers worn over them rather than inside (again, the oilskin trousers don't have to be the expensive lined sort with bibs and braces). In wet dinghies, in cold water, you do need some form of insulation like a wetsuit; but you can make them up yourself from kits for a fraction of the price of a complete suit.

When we asked distinguished yachtsmen and women, for our *Sailing Weekend Book*, what their favourite yachting garment was, they came up with such motley, and cheap, favourites as old Viyella pyjamas worn as insulation under day clothes (Sir Maurice Laing and Blondie Hasler); a mildewed blazer (Mark Brackenbury) and a motorcyclist's hat with earflaps (J.D. Sleightholme). We discovered, from their replies, that really great yachtsmen tend to wear the same sweater for up to 15 years, and that Maurice Griffiths, one of the most inventive and human of classic boat designers, prefers to sail in a well-fitting City bowler hat, because 'in emergency, it serves to bale out the dinghy'. This is an attitude to yachting wear that could save a lot of us a great deal of money.

Finally, the great mass of chandler's wares: the boat gear itself. Again, you can spend thousands on every sort of gizmo, from fancy coloured ropes to amazing non-slip tablemats. And again, you don't necessarily have to. While no-one in their right mind would compromise on solidity and safety – a mooring-line or a lifeline has to be fifty per cent as strong again as you would ever expect it to need to be – there are

plenty of things you can make or improvize (read the yachting magazine practical sketchbook sections, and collect them) and seek out the
Boat Jumble sales. The biggest is at Beaulieu, but there are imitators
everywhere; and shops like Yot Grot at Lymington specialize in
second-hand stuff. Remarkable bargains, even excellent compasses,
turn up here; because, thank heaven, for every broke new boatowner
there will always be another, more prosperous, who is easily seduced
by the glittering newness of each new range, and blithely throws out his
serviceable old stuff. You can enter into the chandlery world at either
level: take your pick.

WHAT ARE LITTLE BOATS MADE OF?

pros and cons

Wood is the traditional construction material for boats. It is still wonderful stuff; pleasant to look at, easy to repair, flexible but strong. It makes a nice creaking noise as you sail along, and gives a warmth to your cabin; when you sit on it with bare legs, it always feels warm and alive.

However, it does rot if you don't look after it. Wooden boats must be protected with either paint or varnish; which means paint or varnish in good condition. One hair of a varnish-brush carelessly left adhering under the coat on a hatch-top can make the whole coat start to lift before the end of the season. One careless knock on a harbour wall, if unrepaired, can let in water which will hide in nooks and crannies for years, happily rotting your precious boat away. Wooden boats have lasted for hundreds of years, but the only people who should really own them are those who have the time, and the willingness, and the modicum of skill, to keep them in good order. Otherwise settle for a certain amount of wooden trim on:

GRP or glassfibre. The great majority of modern boats are made of GRP, and a miraculous material it is. Without too much weight, it can develop immense strength; its good looks are guaranteed by the outer gelcoat (which, eerily enough, is the first part of the boat to be built. They paint it on, inside the mould. So much for the tradition of laying the keel first; today we lay the paint first!) Despite the recent scare about 'osmosis' – in which the outer gelcoat cracks and crazes and lets in water which forms blisters and threatens the strength of the internal plastic laminate – there are ways to protect against this, and it may in any case not be too serious a problem.

81

However, GRP is cold, clinical, plasticky stuff to live with. The nicest boats, from Drascombes at the open-boat end of the market, right up to big yachts, use an awful lot of wooden trim to soften their appearance, and put wooden slats down on cockpit seats for comfort. The most popular wood is teak, which needs less maintenance than softer woods, so the loss of convenience is minimal.

Polyethylene/Polyurethane Foam: Several small boats, canoes, and sailboards and car-toppers, are made out of this very strong, tough combination – a sandwich with the buoyant foam substance inside. It is incredibly tough; before the 1986 Southampton Boat Show, I heard, an Optimist dinghy made from this combination fell off a car roofrack on the motorway. It got a chip or two, but was in fit condition to exhibit.

Steel Big yachts (over 30ft at least) are sometimes made of steel. The strength advantages are obvious; the disadvantage is that a vigilant eye is needed, and frequent repainting, especially inside the bilges, to prevent it rusting.

Ferro-cement Again, big yachts are sometimes made by this system, which involves a framework of wire over which the cement mixture is laid. It is strong, and relatively cheap; and there was a great vogue a few years ago for home-builders to do their own ferro hulls, at a huge financial saving. Sadly, quite a few never got finished. If you are buying a second-hand, home-made ferro yacht, for heaven's sake get a surveyor to go over every detail of it. That should apply to any boat, of course, but particularly to a home-built one.

HOW NOT TO BUY A BOAT:

charter and flotilla

'TRY BEFORE YOU BUY' is one of the oldest and wisest saws for any sort of consumer. It is the reason why the BMIF included as a major plank of its 'Get Afloat, Get a Boat' campaign, which began in 1986, the option of 'toe-in-the-water days': sessions when passing members of the public could simply try out a boat, with no obligation, to see how they liked it.

However, you may want a more lengthy trial; or you may not have the sort of life which makes it practical to own a boat. If so, you can still get any sort of boating holiday you want by *chartering*. There is no need to be put off by the expression: it is only a piece of traditional jargon. Charter simply means Hire. There are different ways to go about it.

Inland Waterways There are dozens of companies hiring out boats to explore the inland waterways; the Inland Waterways Association (address in Appendix 1) will let you know who is in business in the area you want to use. It is generally a very simple business; you pay your deposit, the chap from the boatyard takes you on a quick chug up and down the river to demonstrate the controls, and off you go. If you break down, ring them up and they will come and get you. If you bang into another boat, you should be fully insured; but this happens far less often than one would expect. The boats, from our experience, are finished and equipped to a very high standard; a thoroughly pleasant way of getting afloat for the very first time. Some companies have a curious rule about not taking any parties 'all of the same sex', or all under 25; it's worth checking.

Yacht Charter Here the Yacht Charter Association (see Appendix 1) is the trade organization. People chartering yachts which will go to sea are understandably more cautious than those on the Inland Waterways; but

83

if you are over 18 and look reasonably competent, the odds are you will be happily accepted. After a few lessons in sailing, anyone should be fit to take command on a cautious, fair-weather coastal voyage. There will probably be restrictions on how far you can go – for instance, on the South Coast, Poole to Chichester only. These restrictions have been drawn up by people who know the boat, and the waters, better than you. Keep to them. When you get more adventurous, there are bigger boats you can charter, with fewer restrictions.

Skippered Charter The above type of 'self-drive' charter is called, in the jargon, 'bareboat'. It is also possible, for a lot more money, to hire not only a boat but a skipper. This can prove the best way of learning the ropes, for anyone too shy or too grand to go to a sea-school. It might be a wise precaution to meet your skipper first though; and tell him that you want to learn. some of them regard themselves entirely as professional paid hands, not teachers.

Flotilla Sailing We discovered this last year, and fell for it hook, line and sinker even though we have a perfectly good boat of our own. Greek, Turkish, and Yugoslavian waters have lately been colonized by British companies running flotilla holidays; in which a dozen boats sail in company, with a lead-boat carrying a flotilla-skipper, a 'hostess', and a mechanic. There is quite a lot of freedom, or 'independent sailing', when you are allowed to choose your own ports of call and just meet up every few days with the rest for a barbecue and general head-count; the Mediterranean weather is reliably excellent.

Flotillas fulfil two quite different functions. For people who have their own boats at home, or are between boats (perhaps home-building one over several years) it provides a stress-free holiday in warm waters, and in which someone else (the poor old mechanic on the lead boat) is responsible for mending anything on your boat which goes wrong. Even if you like passage-planning and enjoy the rigours of home waters, a fortnight's lotus-eating is very pleasant.

But even more important, because the weather is so nice, the boats so easy to handle, and a reassuring Admiral-figure always available at the end of a radio receiver, flotillas are an ideal way to try out sailing. Especially if not everyone in the family fancies it at first. On one boat in our first YCA flotilla, there was Dad (keen on sailing, but only done it once), Mum (not keen) and daughters (not keen at all). It looked like a recipe for disaster, but in fact they all loved it, and managed to come second in the end-of-holiday passage race.

There are companies running flotillas in home waters, notably Scotland; and there are sailing-schools who run courses very similar to flotillas, only with a strong instructional bias (instructors join your boat for a day at a time, and radio contact is mandatory). But if you have a very reluctant family, the lure of the Mediterranean sun might just be the final spur to get them afloat . . .

APPENDIX I

useful addresses

YACHT AND DINGHY-RACING CLUBS

A booklet 'Clubs for Newcomers' (price £0.50 including post and packing) is available from the Royal Yachting Association. They also produce a list of affiliated yacht clubs and a list of class associations (each cost £1.70 including postage and packing). Both obtainable from the Membership Branch at Gillingham.

BOATLINE

The BMIF, as part of its 'Get Afloat, Get a Boat' campaign, has installed a Boatline. Ring 0932 45890 and they will answer any of your questions about finding a boat and getting afloat.

USEFUL ADDRESSES

Admiralty Charts & Hydrographic Publications
Hydrographer to the Navy, Taunton, Somerset TA1 2DN. Tel: (0823) 87900
British Hire Cruiser Federation
Canals & Rivers: Association of Pleasure Craft Operators, 35a High Street, Newport, Salop TF10 8JW
Norfolk Broads: The Broadlands Owners Association, Sunway House, Oulton Broad, Lowestoft, Suffolk
Thames: Thames Hire Cruiser Association, 17 Chudleigh Court, Clockhouse Road, Farnborough, Hants GU14 7UA
Cambridgeshire: Great Ouse Boat Builders & Operators Association, River Mill, School Lane, Eaton Socon, St Neots, Huntingdon, Cambs, PE29 3HF
British Marine Industries Federation (BMIF)
Boating Industry House, Vale Road, Oatlands, Weybridge, Surrey. Tel: (0932) 54511
British Waterways Board
Melbury House, Melbury Terrace, London NW1. Tel: 01-262 6711

Cruising Association
Ivory House, St. Katharines Dock, World Trade Centre, London E1 9AT Tel: 01-481 0881

H.M. Coastguard
Dept of Transport, Marine Division, Sunley House, 90–93 High Holborn, London WC1V 6LP Tel: 01-405 6911

Island Cruising Club
Salcombe, Devon, TQ8 8DR. Tel: (054 884) 3481

Jubilee Sailing Trust (sailing for the disabled)
Atlantic Road, Eastern Docks, Southampton, SO1 1GB. Tel: (0703) 6318388

Meteorological Office
London Road, Bracknell, Berkshire RG12 2SZ Tel: (0344) 420242

National Federation of Sailing Schools
Lymington Seamanship & Navigation Centre, 21 New St, Lymington, Hants, SO41 9BH. Tel: (0590) 77601

National Yacht Harbours Association (NYHA)
Hardy House, Somerset Road, Ashford, Kent TN24 8EW. Tel: (0233) 43837. Telex 966241

Ocean Cruising Club (Geoff Hales)
6 Creek End, Emsworth, Hants, PO10 7EX. Tel: (0243) 373756

Old Gaffers Association (W A Brown Esq)
Wheal-Cock, Porkellis, Helston, Cornwall TR13 0JS

Royal Institute of Navigation
1 Kensington Gore, London SW7 2AT. Tel: 01-589 5021

Royal National Lifeboat Institution
West Quay Road, Poole, Dorset BH15 1HZ. Tel: (0202) 671133

Royal Ocean Racing Club
20 St James Place, London SW1A 1NN. Tel: 01-629 3608 (Club), 01-493 5252

Royal Yachting Association (RYA)
Victoria Way, Woking, Surrey GU21 1EQ. Tel: (048-62) 5022

Royal Yachting Association (Membership Branch)
Gillingham, Dorset, SP8 4PQ. Tel: 07476 3287

Sports Council
16 Upper Woburn Place, London WC2H 0QP. Tel: 01-388 1277. Telex 27830

Yacht Brokers, Designers & Surveyors Association
Wheel House, 5 Station Road, Liphook, Hants, GU30 7DW. Tel: (0428) 722322. Telex 477265 A/B BARQUE G. Contact: Mrs Rae Boxall – Co. Sec.

Yacht Charter Association
60 Silverdale, New Milton, Hants BH25 7DE. Tel: (0425) 619004.
Contact: Mr Don Howard – Sec.

APPENDIX II

yachting & sailing magazines

YACHTING MONTHLY (Monthly)
Editor: Andrew Bray
Room 2209
Kings Reach Tower
Stamford Street
London
SE1 9LS

Famous for articles on interesting cruises and advice on offshore seamanship.

YACHTING WORLD (Monthly)
Editor: Dick Johnson
Quadrant House
The Quadrant
Sutton
Surrey
SM2 5AS

Covers the world of offshore cruising and racing with features on the latest yacht design and new equipment, aimed at the more affluent owner.

YACHTS & YACHTING (Fortnightly)
Editor: Peter Cook
196 Eastern Esplanade
Southend-on-Sea
Essex
SS1 3AB

For the racing enthusiast. Articles and regular features on all types of racing from dinghies to offshore – with results and race reports.

MOTOR BOAT & YACHTING (Monthly)
Editor: Alex McMullen
Quadrant House
The Quadrant
Sutton
Surrey
SM2 5AS

Covers every aspect of power-driven yachts – design, engines, seamanship – and also has articles on everything from power boating to motor cruising.

PRACTICAL BOAT OWNER (Monthly)
Editor: George Taylor
Westover House
West Quay Road
Poole
Dorset
BH15 1JG

Full of hints and advice on all aspects of sailing with special emphasis on DIY and running a boat on an economy budget.

WOODEN BOAT (Bi-monthly)
Editor: Jonathan Wilson
PO Box 78
Brooklin
Maine 04616
USA

An American magazine available in the UK devoted to wooden boats – building, restoration and design.

ON BOARD (Monthly)
60 Station Road
Draycott
Derbyshire
DE7 3AB

Covers the world of sailboarding.

APPENDIX III

Useful books

The Sailing Lifestyle John Rousmaniere (Nautical Books)

This is Sailing Richard Creagh-Osborne (Nautical Books)

This is Complete Windsurfing Ulrich Stanciu (Nautical Books)

The New Laser Sailing Dick Tillman and Dave Powlinson (Nautical Books)

Pass your Yachtmaster's David Fairhall (Nautical Books)

Practical Yacht Navigator (Revised Fourth Edition) Kenneth Wilkes (Nautical Books)

Competent Crew/Day Skipper: A companion to the RYA course Pat Langley-Price and Philip Ouvrey (Adlard Coles Ltd)

Start to Navigate Conrad Dixon (Adlard Coles Ltd)

The Sailing Dictionary; A Comprehensive Reference Book to Modern Sailing Terms Joachim Schult (Adlard Coles Ltd)

The Colour Book of Knots Floris Hin (Nautical Books)

Instant Weather Forecasting A Watts (Adlard Coles Ltd)

Buying or Selling a Boat Colin Jarman (Adlard Coles Ltd)

Boat Owners Practical Dictionary Denny Desoutter (Hollis & Carter)

Dinghy & Boardsailing Weather A Watts (Nautical Books)

Shell Book of Inland Waterways Hugh McKnight (David & Charles)

Stanford's Sailing Companion R J F Riley (Stanford Maritime Ltd)

The Sailing Weekend Book Paul Heiney & Libby Purves (Nautical Books)

Where to Launch Your Boat Diana Goatcher (Barnacle Marine)

APPENDIX IV

Royal Yachting Association training schemes and certificates

THE RYA NATIONAL DINGHY SAILING SCHEME

Provides an introduction to the sport. Basic courses for adults or children may be followed by a range of endorsements according to your interest:

RYA Junior Certificates A practical introduction to sailing for youngsters

RYA National Dinghy Sailing Certificate A sound introduction to the sport of dinghy sailing

Both the above include practical skills such as rowing, paddling, coming alongside, making fast, handling boats ashore, securing to trolleys, storage, rigging, setting sails according to conditions, sailing in various conditions, rules of the road, righting capsized dinghies, recovering Man Overboard, and First Aid; onshore teaching includes basic names and functions of boat parts, ropework, safety principles, distress procedures and understanding of tides. These courses can lead on to either:

Seamanship 1 Endorsement A development of boat-handling and seamanship skills. By the end of the course, the successful sailor will have a competent, safe, practical approach to the sailing of small open boats, and will be capable of sailing and making seamanlike decisions in moderate conditions. Much of the work afloat will be done without instructors aboard. The change in emphasis is towards self-reliance and decision-making by the sailor. Simple meteorology is included.

Seamanship 2 Endorsement Open sea sailing to the highest level of competence. By the end of the course, the successful sailor will be capable of handling a sailing dinghy in strong wind conditions. The extra emphasis is on the teaching of modern and traditional seamanship skills. Charts, buoyage and pilotage in dayboats is included.

These endorsements include more refined sailing skills, such as handling at close quarters, or:

Racing 1 Endorsement An introduction to club dinghy racing. By the end of the course, the successful sailor will have had a sound introduction to racing, including rules, tactics, boat tuning, and strategy planning.

Racing 2 Endorsement A development of racing and an introduction to racing at open meetings and championship level. Includes Spinnaker handling and Physical fitness, also boat trailing.

SPORTSBOAT HANDLING

If you are a powerboat enthusiast or water skier, the RYA National Sportsboat Certificate covers the basic handling skills, maintenance and background knowledge in a two-day course. The Rescue Boat endorsement is particularly suited to those involved in sailing club rescue boat duties, but is widely used by other groups. The course includes launch and recovery, care of trailer, preparation of safety equipment, lines, and fenders; handling under way, trim, balance, low speed steering, effects of windage, high speed steering, emergency stop, securing and anchoring, Man Overboard, and procedures for disabled craft and for accepting a tow. Fire prevention, tides, rough water handling, basic meteorology, and Rule of the Road are also included.

NATIONAL CRUISING SCHEME

The RYA Cruising Scheme can be entered at any stage. There are five levels:

Competent Crew A useful person to have aboard. Basic seamanship, navigation, safety, understanding of tides. Five days practical course, 100 miles seatime including 4 night hours. No examination.

RYA Day Skipper/Watch Leader Can handle a small cruising yacht in local waters. More navigation included than above; 10 days, 200 miles seatime, 8 night hours required. No examination.

RYA/DoT Coastal Skipper Can manage a cruising yacht on coastal passages by day or night. Navigation and meteorology taught. 5 day practical course, 20 days seatime, 400 miles, and 12 night hours required. Oral examination for holders of course completion certificates; practical for others.

RYA/DoT Yachtmaster (Offshore) Competent to skipper a cruising yacht on any passage which does not require astro-navigation. Theory as above; 50 days seatime, 2,500 miles, and five passages over 60 miles (two as skipper); also two overnight passages. Practical examination.

RYA/DoT Yachtmaster (Ocean) An experienced yachtsman, competent to skipper a yacht on passages of any length, anywhere in the world. Astronavigation and worldwide meteorology included. Open only to Yachtmasters Offshore. Ocean passage required, and assessment made of sights taken at sea, also written examination.

Further information available from The Royal Yachting Association, Victoria Way, Woking, Surrey GU21 1EQ